- I N   T H E   H I L L S   O F   T U S C A N Y   -

Library of Congress Cataloging-in-Publication Data

Phillips, Kyle Meredith, Jr.
      In the hills of Tuscany : recent excavations at the Etruscan
site of Poggio Civitate (Murlo, Siena) / by Kyle M. Phillips, Jr.

          p. cm.
      Includes Annotated Bibliography by Ingrid E.M. Edlund-Berry and Kyle M. Phillips, Jr.
      ISBN 0–934718–96–2
      1. Poggio Civitate Site (Italy) 2. Excavations (Archaeology)—Italy—Siena
(Province) 3. Etruscans—Italy—Siena (Province) 4. Etruria—Antiquities. I. Title.
      DG70.P64P49 1992
945'.58—dc20   92–27557
                                                         CIP

THE PUBLICATION OF THIS VOLUME WAS MADE POSSIBLE
BY A GENEROUS GRANT FROM THE GETTY TRUST.

ADDITIONAL FUNDING WAS PROVIDED BY THE ALWYN M. COTTON FOUNDATION,
THE CUMMER FUND OF BRYN MAWR COLLEGE, AND MANY FAMILY MEMBERS,
FRIENDS, AND COLLEAGUES OF THE AUTHOR.

Design and Production: Bagnell & Socha
Printing: Cypher Press
Landscape photos copyrighted by William Hirsch
Frontispiece photo by Chris Williams

Contents

—

Figures

———

Foreword

KYLE MEREDITH PHILLIPS, JR. SERVED AS A RESEARCH ASSOCIATE IN the Mediterranean Section of The University Museum of Archaeology and Anthropology from 1972 until his death in 1988. During that time, Kyle worked on several publication projects for the Museum—three volumes of the *Corpus Vasorum Antiquorum* (co-authored with Ann Ashmead) including all of the red-figure pottery in the Museum's collections (in preparation), articles for *Expedition* magazine, and this book on the excavations at Poggio Civitate near Murlo, Siena in the hills of Tuscany.

Kyle Phillips submitted the final version of this manuscript a few short days before his death. His book will stand as a unique assessment of the site of Murlo by the man who excavated the site and studied its material for more than 20 years. He pondered the significance of Murlo and its function, and debated his thoughts and theories with many colleagues over the years—by correspondence, phone, or over a cup of coffee in the Museum Cafe.

A most unusual part of the author's plan was to offer with the text a complete and annotated bibliography from the beginning of the work at Murlo up to publication date of all references to the material in any primary or secondary publication. This invaluable part of the volume has been compiled by Ingrid Edlund-Berry, working closely with Kyle Phillips while he lived and updating the list thereafter through 1992. This bibliography makes the volume unparalleled in archaeological publication.

It has been a special trust for the Museum to publish this book posthumously without further recourse to Kyle's lively and wide-ranging intelligence in producing the final product. Many people have played vital roles in the final stages of this publication and in maintaining the standards that the author himself would have insisted upon.

Mrs. Kyle M. Phillips, Jr. and Kyle M. Phillips, III have been extremely helpful in providing additional photographs

(many of the photographs in the volume were taken by Kyle M. Phillips, III) and in their patience and support of this book. Eric Nielsen has kindly supplied additional photographic material from the Murlo Excavation Archives. David and Francesca Ridgway generously wrote the introduction for the book, helping to place Murlo in the context of our knowledge of the Etruscan world. Several people who worked at the site were always willing to answer my questions or offer their friendly support—Richard De Puma, Penny Small, and Greg Warden.

Ingrid Edlund-Berry gave unstintingly of her time in supplying necessary editorial comments, checking photographic identifications, and proofreading text and bibliography. Without her dedication, knowledge, and guidance, this book would have been much more difficult to complete. Lucy Shoe Meritt, to whom so many of us already owe such a large debt for her scholarship and teaching, has been the spirit behind this project—her wisdom and graciousness were invaluable.

KAREN BROWN VELLUCCI
Managing Editor
The University Museum
of Archaeology and Anthropology
June 1993

Preface

DAVID AND FRANCESCA RIDGWAY

UNIVERSITY OF EDINBURGH, SCOTLAND – UK

THE PREMATURE DEATH IN 1988 OF KYLE MEREDITH PHILLIPS, JR., robbed archaeology of a fine and generous scholar, a brilliant fieldworker and an inspiring teacher. This book contains his final account of the excavations at Poggio Civitate, the Etruscan site near Siena in central Italy that was never far from his thoughts in the last twenty-two years of his life. The evidence and the conclusions to which it leads are set out here in what he knew to be some of the last pages that he would write: they have unique status, and we should like to express just a little of the gratitude with which we remember their author by reviewing the effect that the emergence of Poggio Civitate under his guidance has had on Etruscan studies.

In 1966, when work began at Poggio Civitate, scholars and the general public were well and truly aware of the Etruscans—the people who, in Cato the Elder's words, "ruled nearly the whole of Italy" before the spread of Roman domination. The picture was far from complete. Two hundred years of excavation, not always scientific, had been largely confined to the cemeteries and sanctuaries that surrounded the main Etruscan cities. The latter, mentioned with respect and awe by Greek and Roman authors, had been effectively obliterated by centuries of Roman and later habitation, which in many cases continued without a break to modern times. On this somewhat limited showing, Etruscan culture, though in many ways original and undoubtedly interesting, had so much in common with that of contemporary Archaic and Classical Greece as to appear dependent on it—and therefore second-rate in comparison. Indeed, it was not until 1975 that a modern scholar felt able to write about the Etruscans in terms of "a ranking civilization which played an important role in the history of the world, both in its own time and through its influence on Rome" (BONFANTE 1975:1).

A decade earlier, however, nothing was more appropriate than the thorough exploration of an Etruscan site which, unlike the major cities, was small enough to be profitably excavated and published within a reasonable time by a university team. At Poggio Civitate, Kyle Phillips hoped to find the remains of ordinary houses, shops, yards, workplaces, and perhaps a modest public building: the kind of context that would provide some much-needed basic information about everyday life in a typical Etruscan community. In the event, the site turned out to be neither modest nor typical. Its buildings are anything but ordinary, and there are accordingly a good many questions about Etruscan daily life on which they shed little or no light. Any disappointment in this respect is far outweighed by the new, detailed, and reliably excavated answers that Poggio Civitate *does* provide—especially to artistic and historical questions that had barely been formulated when the first spade went into the ground there.

Even so, it has to be admitted that Poggio Civitate is not one of the great landmarks of the ancient world. None of the inscriptions found there gives us its Etruscan name, nor can it be identified with any of the Etruscan centers mentioned by the Greek and Roman authors.

Yet the building complex described and illustrated in this book is one of the earliest and largest known in Archaic central Italy. The evidence of excavation shows that around 530 B.C. it was deliberately dismantled, ritually buried, and delimited by a long earthen mound (*agger*) to show that it should never again be inhabited or otherwise used by man. Whatever its function (see below), it most probably fell victim to the expanding power of nearby Clusium (modern Chiusi), the Etruscan city that, under the *lucumo* Porsenna, was at this time extending its influence as far as Rome.

Happily for archaeology, the dramatic end of Poggio Civitate preserved the plan of the buildings almost intact, along with a larger proportion than usual of their structural and decorative elements. Right from the beginning of the excavation, the finds included fragments—now numbered in thousands—of the specialized terracotta revetments that had once adorned the wooden frame of the roofs that covered the rubble and half-timbered pisé or mudbrick structures. This kind of material had long been known as a characteristic feature of monumental buildings in central Italy during the Archaic, Classical, and Hellenistic periods, long after the Greeks (both at home and in their Western colonies) had abandoned terracotta in favor of richer and more permanent marble or limestone roofings.

What sort of buildings were decorated with architectural terracottas? Before excavations began at Poggio Civitate, this was not a question that was asked by experts: they were sure that only temples were entitled to such treatment, a conviction that was reflected in the title of Arvid Andrén's still standard corpus of the terracottas in question (*Architectural Terracottas from Etrusco-Italic Temples*, Lund 1940). But the architectural terracottas from Poggio Civitate were soon recognized as different in many respects from those classified by Andrén. And the overall plan that was emerging had nothing in common with that of any temple, Greek or Tuscan, anywhere in Italy: it shows a large courtyard, nearly square, enclosed by four connected wings, faced with porticoes and covered by the sloping roofs to which the terracottas had once been attached.

It was not long before these new discoveries became widely known. Kyle Phillips published regular and informative preliminary reports on progress at his site; and these were soon joined by detailed accounts of the various groups of material that he had assigned for study to individual members of his team (a complete list of these excavation reports and primary studies is included in the impressive Annotated Bibliography that appears elsewhere in this book). Moreover, after only four years' work, he accepted an invitation from the Archaeological Superin-

tendency in Florence to present his findings in an exhibition in Florence and Siena that will long be remembered as a watershed in modern perceptions of the Archaic period in Northern Etruria (catalogue, *POGGIO CIVITATE* 1970). At this stage, such a vast and rich complex, dated to the early sixth century B.C., could only be interpreted as a sanctuary; Kyle Phillips soon qualified this notion with the suggestion that it might have had a federal function as the meeting place of a local religious or political league (STOCKHOLM 1972:103; cf. PHILLIPS 1985:14, note 13).

Meanwhile, another breakthrough was still to come. After the 1970 exhibition, excavation revealed that the remains of an earlier building were buried underneath the Archaic complex. Similar to the latter in shape and layout, it had been constructed between 675 and 650 B.C. and accidentally destroyed by fire around 610, to be replaced shortly afterward by its Archaic successor. This Orientalizing building had also been covered with terracotta tiles and figured ornaments: an entirely new dimension to existing knowledge of seventh-century Etruscan architecture—and society. As luck would have it, contemporary excavations conducted by the Swedish Institute in Rome at Acquarossa di Ferento in Southern Etruria were revealing other examples of Orientalizing architectural terracottas; most of them could safely be attributed to relatively simple, and certainly private, houses. Such an attribution was clearly out of the question at Poggio Civitate. There too, however, the "sanctuary hypothesis" was being seen as increasingly less appropriate to the Archaic complex, especially in the simplified version that had achieved wide currency in spite of the excavator's subsequent modifications of his original definition.

Thanks to Kyle Phillips' generosity in sharing his findings, many interpretations were offered by scholars who had not been associated with Poggio Civitate and who did not feel inhibited either by the obviously incomplete publication of the evidence or even by the unfinished state of the excavation. In some quarters, a number of these suggestions have crystallized into the dogma that the Archaic building complex at Poggio Civitate was the "private" palazzo or residence of a powerful lord (bibliography, PHILLIPS 1983:21, note 5; comment, NIELSEN AND PHILLIPS 1977A:85). In our view, the approach of the late Ranuccio Bianchi Bandinelli was much wiser: "This complex should not have existed in the Archaic period. But it did. What can we do? How can we interpret it?" (Siena 1985:98). We ourselves trust the judgment of Kyle Phillips and his colleagues at the site. Their broad definition, well expounded in the following pages, of the Orientalizing and Archaic complexes as "Meeting Halls" for a "Northern League" from about 675 to 550/530 B.C. seems to fit not only the evidence of excavation and the local geographical setting but also the current (and now better-informed) understanding of how early Etruscan society might have worked.

Naturally, as in any serious scholarly enquiry, all conclusions must be regarded as provisional and constantly subject to revision in the light of new evidence acquired as the investigation proceeds. At the same time, the discussion and even head-on collision of diverging opinions is intrinsically useful in advancing knowledge and comprehension. Thus the diagnosis of the general plan of the complex at Poggio Civitate as a residence rather than a sacred place generated new hypotheses regarding the origin and development of the Regia in Rome. Meanwhile, certain specific features of the plan, and its size, have suggested a possible derivation from Near Eastern models that apparently did not reach Etruria through Hellenic mediation (e.g., TORELLI 1985). If this is true, it tells us a lot about direct contacts between Northern Etruria and the regions beyond the Aegean to which Annette Rathje (1988) has traced the origin of the early "banquet culture" in Etruria, as shown on the Archaic frieze-plaques at Poggio Civitate—which now provide the oldest representation known in Italy of a reclining banquet.

The coherent assemblage of the Archaic architectural terracottas (ranging from the highly informative frieze-plaques to the imposing seated figures with wide-brimmed "cowboy" hats) has generated extensive discussion of their potential social, political, and religious meanings as well as of their artistic worth; speculation under these headings is far from exhausted. The Orientalizing pieces are no less significant. Together with their counterparts from Acquarossa, they add a new phase to the tripartite stylistic and chronological sequence first established by Della Seta (1918) and later codified by Andrén (1940).

In much recent literature, the new Orientalizing architectural terracottas from Northern and Southern Etruria are seen as the result of the introduction into Etruria, from Greece, of a fully formed system of roofing to replace the old thatching of huts; and the credit for this is usually assigned to the semi-legendary figure of Demaratus of Corinth, who is said by some ancient authors to have brought a trio of transparently named craftsmen to Tarquinia around the middle of the seventh century (Ridgway and Ridgway in press). But Eva Rystedt (1983) has shown that, for all their basic structural affinities, the two series of Orientalizing terracottas at Acquarossa and Poggio Civitate are derived from two distinct stylistic trends, represented respectively by the Caeretan pottery tradition in the south and by Northern Etruscan traditions documented in various media, not least in the

finds of pottery, ivory, metal utensils, and ornaments at Poggio Civitate itself. In particular, the cut-out akroteria, both in their "wooden" technique and in their characteristic disposition along the ridge of saddle roofs, recall the appearance of the huts reproduced in many Iron Age funerary models from central Italy (BARTOLONI ET AL. 1987). The resemblance is so close that it is impossible to deny a direct genetic connection with a strong indigenous tradition that is independent of Greek teaching and example—and thus provides much food for thought about the interpretation of other early developments, spiritual as well as material, in the Etruscan world as a whole.

The parallels recognized by Rystedt between the early terracottas and other artifact categories can be extended to most of the small finds at Poggio Civitate, of both the Orientalizing and the Archaic periods. They all share a distinctive "Northern" flavor, which they have in fact helped to define in the various aspects of its autonomous adaptation of techniques and forms derived from contacts with the Greek world. The area of this world that seems to have been especially active in relation to Clusium and the surrounding area is the Greek colony of Taras (modern Taranto) in Apulia, whence exchanges were effected mainly via the Adriatic Sea and the Apennine passes rather than by the (to us) more familiar Tyrrhenian routes. In addition, the small finds from Poggio Civitate have done much to clarify the socioeconomic dimension of early Etruria. It is clear that this center, far removed from the great coastal cities, was more efficiently organized than would previously have been thought possible: it could produce not only the heavy (and not easily transportable) terracottas, but also its own luxury goods (of ivory and bronze, for example) and vast quantities of pottery (including whole banquet sets for dozens of people).

On the wider historical front, the finds from Poggio Civitate are an ideal complement to the exclusively funerary material previously known from the rich cemeteries around Clusium and elsewhere in Northern Etruria, where few Etruscan buildings have survived the ravages of Roman, Medieval, and later settlement. This gap in the local archaeological documentation had long hampered the investigation of the contacts between Etruria and the outside ("uncivilized") world: now, thanks to Poggio Civitate, many more specifically Northern Etruscan features and influences can be recognized wherever they occur.

A particularly interesting set of correspondences has been identified between the figured scenes on the terracotta frieze-plaques from Poggio Civitate and those on the distinctive situlas (buckets) and other decorated bronzes made in northeast Italy, the Alps, and beyond from the seventh century B.C. onward. The Etruscan techniques, fashions, and ideas borrowed by the northerly "Situla Art people" from the Northern Etruscan repertoire have been reviewed by Larissa Bonfante (1981:1–81), whose "Etruscan's eye view" of Situla Art contrasts strikingly with another southerly perspective presented only a few years earlier (BOARDMAN 1971). Bonfante used a series of remarkably similar representations of dress and furniture at Poggio Civitate and on the situlas around the head of the Adriatic to confirm the status of Clusium and its neighbors as the missing link at the beginning of the chain of northward transmission. We now know much more than we did before about the circumstances in which the Etruscans introduced their European contemporaries to the use of the human figure in narrative art, to wine making, to urban life, and above all to writing—all vital civilizing elements that the Etruscans themselves had long since acquired from their own early Greek and Levantine visitors.

The Etruscan site at Poggio Civitate is one of the most significant structural complexes ever excavated by a foreign archaeological mission in Italy. The evidence that has told specialists and the general public so much about the people who used these extraordinary buildings is now permanently displayed in its own Antiquarium at Murlo, the modern *comune* to which Poggio Civitate belongs. For those who can make the trip, and for the many more who cannot, Kyle Phillips has left this lucid and effective summary of the story so far. It is an exhilarating narrative of discovery and of progressively better explanation. It is also something more. As we have tried to show, Poggio Civitate has made an outstanding contribution to the deeper knowledge and wider appreciation of the formative early stages in one of the great civilizations of the world. The following pages are a new chapter in our own history.

recording, and restoration. Academic credit was awarded and fees were charged; however, the site retained its essential nature as a training ground for young archaeologists. Even though Dr. Nielsen is now [1988] Dean of Humanities at Trinity University in San Antonio, Texas, Bowdoin College continues to sponsor the training of students at Murlo.

Preliminary reports in the *American Journal of Archaeology, Dialoghi di Archeologia, Notizie degli Scavi di Antichità*, and *Studi Etruschi* have kept the archaeological public posted on the site; in addition, specialized reports and studies have integrated that work with previous discoveries. Murlo material has been displayed in a number of shows, starting with the exhibitions held during the summer of 1970 at Florence and Siena. In late 1972 and early 1973 the exhibit was on display in Stockholm in honor of His Late Majesty, Gustaf VI Adolf, the King of Sweden. Another exhibition, organized by Guglielmo Maetzke and Ranuccio Bianchi Bandinelli, was housed in the "Sala Marcolina" of the Palazzo Comunale of Siena between 1973 and 1985. Murlo artifacts were included in the show of precious Etruscan objects held at Arezzo in 1984. A large show was displayed in Siena for the "Year of the Etruscans" celebrated throughout Italy in 1985. Finally, in July of 1988, a museum of material from Poggio Civitate was opened at Murlo itself.

Many scholars have been involved with the publication of the site and much more remains to be done. The present review will show that my own interest has been primarily with the architectural terracottas and the architecture of the site, even though pottery has been a second, very important concern. As it stands now, I am primarily responsible for the work carried out in the Archaic Complex and for much of the material found under its floor levels. Nielsen is publishing the areas he excavated to the south of the Archaic Complex and will be primarily responsible for other material from the Orientalizing period. Naturally, we have discussed problems of publication and have shared in assigning topics to other scholars.

This article, accompanied by the thoroughly and carefully documented bibliography drawn together by Ingrid Edlund-Berry, reflects a series of thoughts which I have been mulling over for a number of years. It is hoped that these will help others see the site and its problems more clearly. In no way do I see my ideas as final solutions; they are suggestions for interpreting what has been thus far found and may be changed in the future, particularly in the light of future excavation.

The work at Poggio Civitate has always been fascinating and I thank Drs. Giacomo Caputo, Guglielmo Maetzke, and Francesco Nicosia of the Florence

Archaeological Museum, and Maurizio Morviducci, the former mayor of Murlo, for their generous backing. I have enjoyed and profited by work with students and staff members at the site. I take this opportunity to thank Hans Lindén S.A.R., whose extensive work restoring Swedish cultural monuments adds great weight to his opinions, and who carefully and lovingly drew the remains of the Archaic Meeting Hall and worked out aspects of its complex restoration. Our work owes much to his exacting craft and to his precision as an architect. I give thanks to all Murlo staff members, and especially to Erik O. Nielsen, who has shared the many ups and downs of the excavations at Poggio Civitate with me since 1970, first as a student and now as Co-Director of the Excavations and Field Director, and to Ingrid Edlund-Berry, who has assisted in so many publications of the site. The memory of Professor Ranuccio Bianchi Bandinelli will always be associated with Poggio Civitate, and I recall his many visits with pleasure.

Certain costs of producing this study have been met by the Cummer Publication Fund of Bryn Mawr College. A grant from the Agnes Milliken Foundation gave me the leisure to write the study and to test out its many conclusions. The very important editing of this manuscript was kindly carried out by Karen Brown Vellucci of The University Museum of Archaeology and Anthropol-ogy. I thank her, a former student, a colleague, and a friend. Mistakes are mine, but there would have been many, many more had she, Ann Ashmead, Donald White, and Ingrid Edlund-Berry not taken this article in hand. Photographs are by Kyle Meredith Phillips, III, or by various excavation photographers.

Field work, under the direction of Erik Nielsen, continues at the site, and it will be many years before Poggio Civitate has been fully explored. Future scientific study and the publications resulting from them may change many of our opinions about the site; however, this review of past work on Poggio Civitate and the bibliography should assist others in reaching their own opinions about this fascinating Etruscan center.

Kyle Meredith Phillips, Jr.
Co-Director of the Murlo Excavations
Research Associate, The University Museum
of Archaeology and Anthropology
The University of Pennsylvania
July 1988

Editor's Postscript: Since 1988 excavations have continued at Poggio Civitate, under the direction of Professor Erik O. Nielsen, Vice-President for Academic Affairs at the University of Evansville. As indicated in sections I and II of the Annotated Bibliography, several primary and secondary publications have appeared, including three articles by Phillips, which were in press or in manuscript form at the author's death (Phillips 1989A, 1989B and 1990). As predicted by Phillips, the discussions about Poggio Civitate continue to intrigue us, and more publications are forthcoming; those known by title are listed in section IV of the Annotated Bibliography.

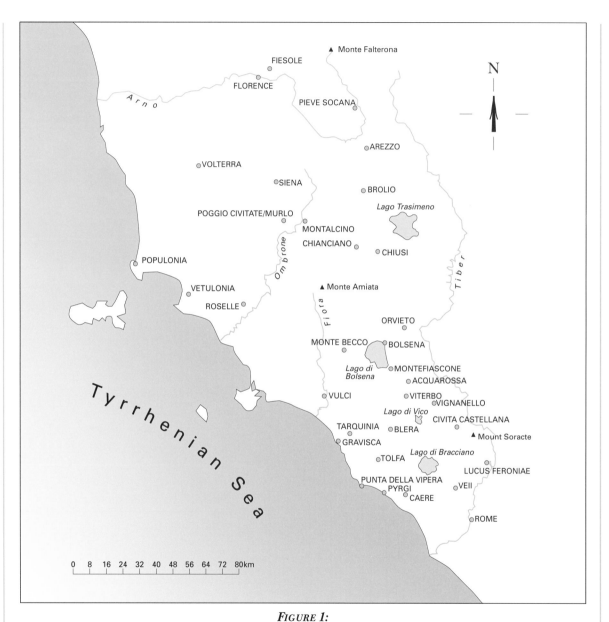

FIGURE 1:

Map of Etruria, showing location of Poggio Civitate and Montalcino.
After Edlund 1987, 32, figure 2.

Introduction[†]

During the summer of 1965 Katherine McBride, President of Bryn Mawr College, authorized me to look for an archaeological site within Tuscany that could function as a training ground for students, either undergraduates considering entering graduate school in archaeology or graduate students already committed to the field. No restrictions were placed on the type of site to be selected; however, we hoped that it would be small enough for students to supervise the excavations, undertake the cataloguing and documentation of the finds, and finally, through their classes and seminars at the college, prepare the preliminary publications of the excavated materials. Following the suggestions of Professors Richard Stillwell and Erik Sjöqvist of Princeton University, I decided to look for a site that could be excavated with a minimum of heavy equipment.

During the summer of 1963 I had the good fortune to excavate a limited number of burials in two small groups of Hellenistic tombs within the bounds of the estates of Malignano (Comune of Rosia) and Frosini (Comune of Chiusdino), which lie to the west of Siena within the ancient territory of Volterra. Professor Ranuccio Bianchi Bandinelli (whose early research included a monumental study on Chiusi,[1] a survey of Siena and its territory,[2] and an edition of *Carta archeologica d'Italia* for the area of Siena[3]) observed this work with interest. When I discussed our excavation plans with him, he suggested that we look closely at sites within the vicinity of Siena because little systematic work had been carried out within that area even though it was known to be rich in objects from the Neolithic to the late Roman Period. He did not recommend a particular site; rather he referred to his early surveys and urged me to visit each major center before making a selection (Fig. 1).

By the end of the summer of 1965 I had selected four sites for possible excavation. At the head of the list was Poggio Civitate ("The Inhabited Hill"), an isolated wooded hill within the confines of

† With minor editorial corrections, the text and brief footnotes read as they were written in 1988. For the bibliographical references in the footnotes, see the bibliography on pp. 95–99. For complete bibliographical information about specific objects, see the excavation reports (marked with * in the bibliography), the primary publications (marked with ** in the bibliography), or the exhibition catalogue for the Year of the Etruscans (SIENA *CP*, 1985; note, however, that there are some misprints in the catalogue entries).—In order to inform the readers of new discoveries and additional bibliography, I have included some additional information in brackets. Books and articles are referred to by the abbreviations used in the Annotated Bibliography, sections I–IV, for which see pages 107–140.—Ingrid E.M. Edlund-Berry, November 1992.

Murlo, a comune to the south of Siena (Figs. 2 and 3). Attention was drawn to that site by a number of pieces on display in the Siena Archaeological Museum. The most interesting material dated to the early Archaic period—bronze buckles inlaid with iron, a bronze helmet, an iron spear point, and a few fibulae.[4] Poggio Civitate, situated between the Sienese clay district (the Sienese *crete*) to the south of Siena and the metal-bearing mountains that stretch nearly to the coast, is an isolated hill to the north of the Ombrone River (Fig. 4). It and Montalcino, to the south of the Ombrone, dominate that river pass which is a natural route between central Tuscany and the Mediterranean sea. Poggio Civitate and Montalcino are at the center of the territory between Roselle, Populonia, Volterra, Fiesole, Arezzo, Chiusi, and Vulci. Their strategic location, close to the hub of Northern Etruria, intrigued me. I decided that I had to look more closely at Poggio Civitate, since that site could be explored, while the ancient remains of Montalcino lay under the present city, beyond any hope of excavation.

At the end of August I went to Murlo in order to find out as much as possible about Poggio Civitate. Fortunately, Maurizio Morviducci, the mayor of the comune, immediately understood the archaeological problems and introduced me to a number of older citizens of the town. One, a woman of about seventy-five, remembered seeing the bronze helmet (Fig. 5) and iron spear point from the Siena Archaeological Museum soon after they were found. She said they came from the top of Poggio Aguzzo, a small appendage to Poggio Civitate, and were found while trenches were being dug for planting grapes early in this century. Her information confirmed the idea that the pieces were from tombs and suggested that Poggio Civitate was the site of an early occupation. (The local painter Dario Neri had drawn Bianchi Bandinelli's attention to the pieces, which had then been passed on to the Soprintendenza at Florence.) Because I knew of no case in which the Etruscans carried their dead up a mountain for burial, I reasoned that the tombs on Poggio Aguzzo were part of the cemetery for a settlement that must have been on the top of Poggio Civitate. The dead would have been carried from that center to the necropolis along the slightly undulating plateau which formed the top of the two hills. It seemed logical that the Archaic occupation on Poggio Civitate could be found because the hill was relatively small and totally contained. Covered by scrub trees and thick underbrush, its slopes rise to an isolated upper plateau, whose highest point is 365 m. above sea level.[5] Therefore, permission to excavate was formally requested through the Florence Archaeological Museum and its director, Professor Giacomo Caputo.

FIGURE 2:
View of the piazza of Murlo

FIGURE 3:
View of the piazza of Murlo.

FIGURE 4:
Poggio Civitate.

FIGURE 5:
Bronze helmet.
Height, 0.20 m.

FIGURE 6:
Piano del Tesoro, Trench 1. Photo: W.W. Cummer III.

Part I

EXCAVATIONS IN THE ARCHAIC MEETING HALL

INITIAL WORK ON PIANO DEL TESORO

The initial season at Poggio Civitate started in the late spring of 1966 and continued until late August.[6] Our first task was to explore the plateau on Poggio Civitate with the idea of finding the best spots to sink trial trenches. We had already heard from the workmen hired for that season that two areas of the plateau had particular local names—*Piano del Tesoro* ("the plateau of the treasure") and *Civita Magna* ("the large inhabited place"). Both were at the far end of the hill from Poggio Aguzzo and its necropolis.

W. W. Cummer III organized three days during which the excavation staff thrashed through the thick underbrush looking for signs of occupation. At the end of this exploration he reported that the most interesting point to start excava-

tions was near an unusual earthen mound, an *agger*, measuring approximately 5 m. in width, 3 m. in height, and perhaps 60 m. in length, which separated Piano del Tesoro from Civita Magna.[7] This mound, highest at its center and sloping steeply on its sides, was covered by a layer of irregular large stones placed with no apparent order. One rim fragment of a large impasto pithos, a clay storage jar, protruded from the leafy covering of the mound, and we decided that the piece, because of its particular profile, was either ancient Italic or Etruscan, and not Medieval or modern.[8] We also decided that the mound was man-made, perhaps even ancient, and that our first trial trenches ought to be sunk parallel to it, within Piano del Tesoro.

Trench 1 (Fig. 6) was placed at the northern end of the earthen mound;

Trench 2 was laid out at its southern end. The two trenches were deliberately situated about 60 m. apart. Within hours we knew that we were excavating human occupation. We had to wait four years, however, to discover that both trenches cut into the same monumental building— Trench 1 exposed part of its northern flank[9] and Trench 2 part of its southern.[10]

Trench 1 became the anchor for a network of smaller trenches, designated Piano del Tesoro, Complex 1.[11] This complex was relatively simple to interpret. A well-constructed rubble wall, 1.20 m. in width, ran from the western side of the complex in an eastern direction. A tile layer lay near the surface of the soil immediately to the north of this rubble wall.[12] This layer contained pan and cover tiles, and a number of specialized terracotta revetments including fragments of frieze plaques, lateral simas, antefixes, and akroteria. These architectural terracottas form one of the earliest and most complete sets of Etruscan revetments from the initial years of the Archaic period. Most of the finds were very close to the surface, just below the humus layers deposited by the brushy overgrowth.

Next we sank four small test trenches perpendicular to the rubble wall, which turned out to be a well-constructed foundation wall resting on hardpan and bedrock.[13] Because of these test trenches, we knew that these finds rested on a distinct yellow stratum of sandy earth that had been deliberately smoothed.[14] Later we were to discover that the beaten yellow layers to the south of the rubble foundation walls were earthen floors and that the layers to the north of the foundations walls had also been dressed by hand.[15] Both layers were laid down in antiquity. Because of the very broken nature of the material in the tile fall and because it rested on man-made levels, we decided to excavate horizontally in order to clear the debris on these levels, but not to cut through them again until we had exposed the plan of the entire building. In this way we hoped to lay bare the outline of the building whose wall we had found; furthermore, by excavating horizontally rather than vertically, we were assured of not mixing the strata, which were difficult to distinguish.

The reader will recognize that this review article follows the system of excavation. The Archaic materials, those nearest the surface, are discussed before the earlier Orientalizing occupation. Much of the latter was found *under* the Archaic buildings.

We were immediately perplexed by the paucity of intact objects and the volume of broken pottery and animal bones. The fragmentary nature of the architectural terracottas also seemed curious, as if they had been deliberately smashed and strewn above the earthen floors. The style of these pieces, especially the frieze plaques, suggested a date early in the sixth century B.C. for the building they adorned.

Thus, by the end of the first season we were in a position to suspect that we had found an important northern architectural complex of the early Archaic period decorated with unusual architectural terracottas, even though we could only postulate its function. Because of the number and quality of the terracottas, we decided that we had hit upon a sanctuary dating to the early years of the sixth century B.C. Until the excavations at Murlo and Acquarossa proved that terracotta revetments could adorn both public and private structures, anyone who found a frieze plaque, etc., assumed that it adorned a sacred structure. Our work was later to upset this long-standing theory.

SUBSEQUENT RESULTS

Layout of the Archaic Meeting Hall

By 1971 we had cleared enough of the building complex, later dated on the evidence of Greek pottery to the years just before or after 600 B.C., to present the central element of its monumental plan (Fig. 7);[16] we had decided that it was not an Etruscan Temple. One problem of the excavations at Poggio Civitate has been what to call the various buildings. The generic term, Archaic Building Complex, has been given to the major Archaic structures. After extensive analyses of the remains of the site, I have labeled the central unit of the Archaic Building Complex the Archaic Meeting Hall because I think that the site was the seat of an Etruscan League. The Archaic Building Complex has also been called "The Upper Building," and the Orientalizing structures sealed under its floor levels were dubbed "The Lower Building." Only in 1985 were we secure enough in certain of its details to publish a nearly complete version of the ground plan of the total Archaic Complex (Fig. 8).[17] One was immediately struck by the monumentality of the building. Its flanks formed a nearly square

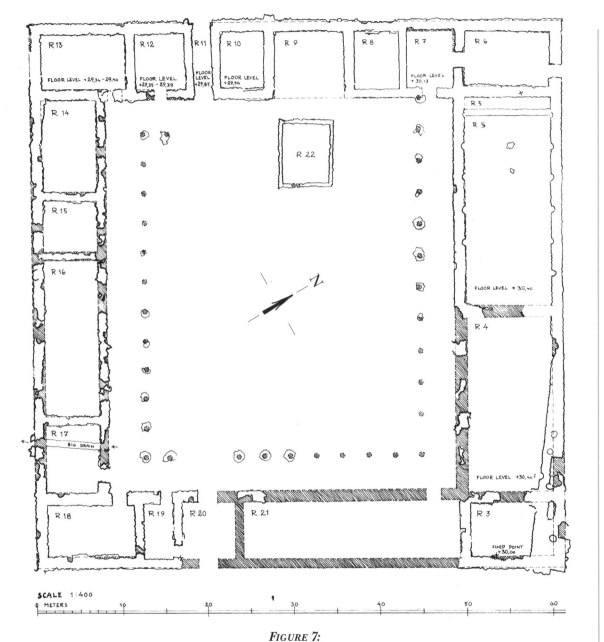

FIGURE 7:

The central unit of the Archaic Meeting Hall on Piano del Tesoro. Drawing and measurements by Hans Lindén. (R = Room in the Archaic Meeting Hall; also = Rectangle in the Orientalizing Meeting Hall.)

structure whose exterior sides measure between 60 m. and 61.85 m. in length. Cummer and Lindén independently worked out that the standard foot at Poggio Civitate was 0.27 m.,[18] a unit which they established through study of the widths of the frieze plaques and simas, both raking and lateral. All three members are 0.54 m. in width, or approximately two feet.[19]

The dominating feature of the Archaic Meeting Hall is a great central court flanked on the north, east, and south by covered porches whose columns or pilasters are indicated by their rubble foundations. The area of the court which includes the porticos is not square; its northern and southern sides measure 43.20 m. (ca. 160 ft.) in length and its western and eastern sides are 40.35 and 40.50 m. (between 149.5 and 150 ft.). This courtyard could have been entered through three doors (Fig. 7). The principal access was probably from the east, through a narrow passage flanked by a guardroom (Rm. 20, Fig. 7). A large, architecturally framed forecourt may have been outside this eastern entrance. A small passage, probably roofed, on the western flank lines up exactly with this eastern entrance (Rm. 11, Fig. 7). It opens onto a narrow walk which runs between the outer wall of the western flank and a *fossa* on that side of the complex. The third entry is from the northern earthen terrace; it passes through the two northern rooms of the western flank and enters the northern porch of the court (Rms. 6 and 7, Fig. 7). This entry, more private and protected than the other two, was probably for the inhabitants of the small house on the earthen terrace between the northern flank of the Archaic Complex and the *fossa* to the north.

On the western side of the central court is a small rectangular structure whose walls are so slight that it probably was an open-air enclosure rather than a roofed building (Rm. 22, Fig. 7). This enclosure is lined up with a room of the western flank which has only three foundation walls; on the side nearest the enclosure no foundations whatsoever existed (Rm. 9, Fig. 7). To the north and south of this three-sided room are rooms of equal size (Rms. 8 and 10, Fig. 7). The enclosure and the three rooms behind it form a coordinated unit which dominates the western side of the courtyard of the Archaic Meeting Hall, and we suspect that this four-roomed unit had a religious function. The open-air enclosure may have been a "templum" in which an official sat to observe birds in the sky, or it could have been a pen to keep animals such as the sacred geese which were maintained on the Capitoline in Rome. Or perhaps the enclosure was simply a pen to house sacrificial animals temporarily.

Another striking feature of the Archaic Meeting Hall's ground plan is the regularity of its four corner rooms (Rms.

3, 6, 13, and 18, Fig. 7). Their equal size ties together the four flanks. The northern flank, because of its greater width, housed the most important rooms of the complex. This flank is carefully balanced on the southern side of the court by a series of smaller rooms which may have been shops. The southern flank and its portico are nearly as wide as the rooms of the northern side. The sophistication and balance of this plan is astounding, and we are convinced that an architect must have laid out its foundations from a measured drawing. If this theory, first put forth by Hans Lindén, is true, we have striking evidence of the vitality and independence of Italic architecture during the late seventh century B.C.

It is nearly impossible to establish the exact function of this building because it has no obvious parallels in Etruscan, Greek, or Near Eastern architecture of the Orientalizing or early Archaic period. I interpret the site as the seat for a Northern League,[20] a loose political-religious organization similar to others known from the ancient world, and have identified the large Archaic Building as the Meeting Hall for such a hypothetical league. (A particularly famous example was the Latin League, whose delegates, citizens of various Latin cities, met regularly on the Aventine Hill in Rome.) I am pleased to note that Ingrid Edlund-Berry identifies Poggio Civitate as a "political sanctuary."[21]

Certain key observations may be drawn from the ground plan alone. Entry is restricted and could have been controlled by shutting the doors on the eastern, western, and northern flanks, much as access to later Roman fora was restricted. Once within the building a large number of people could have carried out, in tranquillity and safety, various activities of the league. For example, some may have gathered in the central court around the unit formed by the three small rooms and the open-air enclosure for religious ceremonies. Others may have attended either civic or religious assemblies held in the large rooms in the northern flank. Such gatherings would have been like those held in the later Basilica Julia or Aemilia in Rome. The southern flank, on the other hand, gives the impression of an area which was more open to the general population at large. Its small rooms suggest shops in which wares were made or sold. The covered portico of this flank could have functioned as a stoa. If general meetings were held in the central court, the three covered porches could also have been refuges from the rain and sun. In broad terms, I think, as expressed previously,[22] that this large and carefully organized series of buildings functioned like a forum. The large open court, surrounded by buildings which served as shops and public halls, would have been ideal for meetings, athletic contests, general assem-

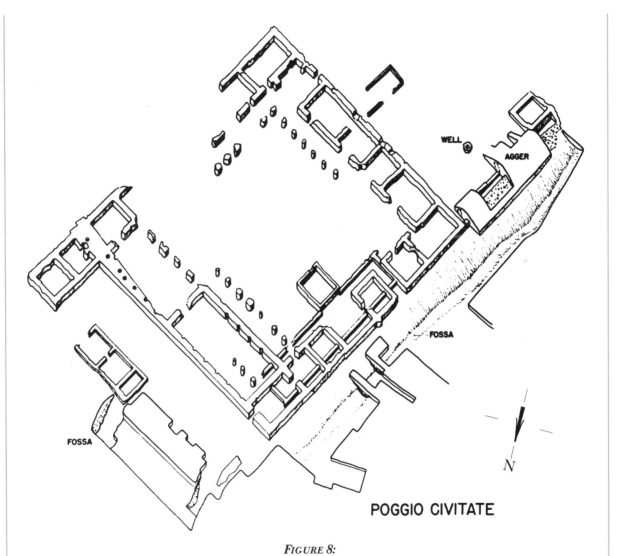

WELL

AGGER

FOSSA

FOSSA

N

POGGIO CIVITATE

FIGURE 8:
Schematic plan of the Archaic Complex on Piano del Tesoro. Drawing by David Peck.

blies and specialized religious functions—the sorts of activities known to have taken place in the Archaic Roman forum, where shops and public buildings also framed the open space.

THE LARGER SETTING

The central rectangular unit of the Archaic Meeting Hall was part of a larger complex.[23] Two rooms (Rms. 1 and 2, Fig. 8) jut north from the eastern end of the northern flank.[24] Their exact function is unknown. To the south is a court whose western enclosure wall is a continuation of the outer wall of the Archaic Meeting Hall's western flank. The southern wall of this well-defended court runs east and has yet to be totally defined; however, Nielsen thinks a room at its western end may have been a defensive tower. Within the court is a well. Nielsen is presently excavating to the south of the Archaic Meeting Hall[25] and to the east of this southern court. There he has cleared a long, stoalike building[26] which contained a tile factory. That structure burned, partially firing many of the tiles laid out to dry under its roof, which may have been revetted with a lateral sima

dating to the second half of the seventh century B.C.[27]

To the north and west of the Archaic Building Complex is a *fossa,* or dry moat, about 3 m. deep and 5 m. wide, which could have kept out wild animals and perhaps delayed wandering brigands or small bands of hostile warriors.

A small house (see Fig. 8), with front, center, and rear rooms, stands on the open area between the outside wall of the northern flank and the *fossa* which runs parallel to that flank.[28] I suspect that this structure is contemporary with the Archaic Building Complex. I now think that it was the residence of the priest or official in charge of the League's Meeting Hall. (A house of such simple form, and not a monumental building like that on Poggio Civitate, could have been the residence of a Northern Etruscan ruler during the early Archaic period.[29] The logical parallel for such a simple abode is the Regia in Rome.)

Although not heavily fortified, the Archaic buildings on Piano del Tesoro were contained and could have been defended against surprise attack. They could also have served as refuges against man or beast, but they were not large enough to hold off large-scale assaults.

CONSTRUCTION METHODS USED IN THE ARCHAIC COMPLEX

T he building methods used in the Archaic structures on Piano del Tesoro are easy to understand. They descend from methods employed during the Orientalizing period at the site. Trenches were dug through the debris of earlier buildings or through virgin soil to hardpan or bedrock. Foundations of rubble stone[30] were laid down, probably as Hans Lindén postulates, from a measured architect's plan. The surface of these foundations was covered by a layer of broken tiles or large pithoi fragments, gathered from the debris of the earlier occupation.[31] These fragments served as the leveling course for the earthen walls which were then constructed on the rubble stone foundations.

All the wall foundations of the Archaic Building Complex (Fig. 6), except those sealed under the earthen

mound, or *agger,* which was piled up when the Archaic Meeting Hall was destroyed, between 550–530 B.C., were within a few centimeters of the surface. Although I suspected that the walls of the Archaic buildings were either of mudbrick or pisé (one mud brick had been found hardened by subsequent firing),[32] no traces of them remained *in situ.* It was not until work started in the *agger* itself that these very fragile and elusive architectural elements were found.

During the 1968 season while we were excavating in the northwest corner of the *agger,* a trench was cut across the exterior foundation of the Archaic Building's northern flank, running perpendicular to that flank. When viewed straight on, the profile of the trench showed the clear outlines of a rammed-earth or pisé wall which was preserved to a height of 1.10 m., or to within 0.30 m. of the *agger's* surface. This wall covered the entire upper surface of the foundation wall.[33] It was darker than the surrounding soil, and its inner surface was coated with a thin layer of light ochre plaster. The exterior of the wall bulged outward from a point about 0.25 m. above the surface of the rubble foundations. At that time I postulated that a wooden beam ran the entire length of the northern flank, resting on the *risega,* or leveling course, which was built into the rubble foundations on their northern side. This beam, which would have measured about 0.25 x 0.25 m., anchored the base of the rammed-earth wall. Vertical and angled wooden beams may have been set into the earthen wall as reinforcement, like those of Medieval and Elizabethan half-timber houses in England. The soil above the *risega,* next to the 0.25 m. high vertical segment of the rammed-earth wall,[34] was of a different texture and color than the surrounding soil, suggesting that fine soil replaced the wood when the beam rotted. (A long stretch of the foundation wall and its *risega* was excavated in 1966.[35])

During the 1969 season we documented other earthen walls, this time interior walls, and discovered that one was a mixture of mudbrick and rammed earth.[36] The vertical facing of that wall was covered with a fine ochre layer of stucco or clay. One cannot help but wonder how these earthen walls were put up. Their width and height demanded that they be built in stages. If wooden forms held the earth in place until it dried, the building technique was a forerunner of the Roman Republican system used for constructing rubble and cement walls.

The earthen walls of the northern flank, perhaps because they were higher and carried a heavier roofing system, had to be reinforced. A series of post holes were cut into the interior faces of the long walls of the large room (Rm. 5) at the western end of the flank (Figs. 7 and 8). These holes are in pairs at regular intervals, one on the northern wall and one on the southern.[37] Wooden columns, probably of oak because that tree has always grown on Poggio Civitate, could have been set into these post holes and, because they were half embedded in the rammed-earth walls, would have sustained the interior face of the earthen walls much as did the wooden lattice work on the exterior. Wooden architraves probably ran the length of the walls of the northern flank; these would have rested directly on the wooden columns or pilasters. The span of ca. 10 m. between northern and southern post holes is not too great for one long oak beam, and I suspect that such beams were used to tie the two walls together.

The weight of the roof of the Archaic Meeting Hall must have been considerable, and a complex system of wooden beams was necessary to support it. Those beams would have been secured to the wooden architraves and to tie beams crossing the northern flank from north to south at each point where pairs of post holes appeared. It is easy to visualize the tie beams, which were the bases of a wooden triangle, whose sides rose diagonally to a ridgepole beam running the entire length of the northern flank. The pitch of the roof, which depended on the angles of these diagonally placed beams, cannot be precisely established. Nor can we establish how far beyond the ends of the triangularly placed rafters these beams extended as the support for overhanging eaves. This series of reinforcing triangles carried the weight of the roof and transferred it directly into the pilasters or columns cut into the earthen walls and set into the post holes. The wooden rafters, described here as triangles, could have been held in place by three or four beams, doweled to their top sides, which ran the entire length of the northern flank. These beams would have been laid parallel to the ridgepole and thus perpendicular to the rafters. These beams in turn may have been covered by wooden boards, which ran from eaves to the ridgepole and met it at right angles. These small boards or beams could have formed a continuous flat surface on which the tiles would have been placed, or the beams themselves may have been spaced so that the edges of the pan tiles rested on them. If the latter were the case, the sides of the pan tile would have been supported by two beams whose centers were slightly more than 0.54 m. apart. (I think it unlikely that pediments terminated the ends of any of the buildings on Piano del Tesoro.) Such an elaborate system of interlocking wooden members for supporting the weight of the terracottas of the roof need cause no surprise. Numerous Archaic tombs at Cerveteri preserve a much more complicated record of Etruscan carpentry techniques than is restored here.

Even with these elaborate wooden supports, the weight of the roof was too great for the building's earthen walls, and the northeast portion of the northern flank's exterior wall gave way. The rubble foundations were thickened and the earthen wall was enlarged, entirely engulfing the wooden pilasters or columns which had been set into the earlier wall.[38] A few of the roof's architectural terracottas may have been replaced during this partial rebuilding of the northern flank.

The Elevation of the Archaic Meeting Hall

The elevation of the Archaic Meeting Hall on Piano del Tesoro is impossible to establish precisely even though a series of solutions can be suggested. The northern flank is the most monumental and most imposing portion of the complex because of the size of its rooms, the width and sturdy nature of its rubble foundations, and the post holes for pilasters cutting into its earthen walls in order to support the roofing system. I think this flank rose to the height of two stories. The large western room of the northern side of the court (Rm. 5, Fig. 7) may have been open from floor to roof, just as were the central naves of many Medieval churches. (The magnificent Romanesque monastic church of Sant'Antimo, one of the most imposing examples of Sienese architecture, which lies between Montalcino and Monte Amiata, is a particularly good example of such a hall rising two or three stories to a wooden roof.) The large eastern room (Rm. 4) within the northern flank perhaps was covered by a second story containing a series of rooms. If the walls of the northern flank rose to the height postulated here, there is the distinct possibility that they were pierced by windows. If this were the case, a clerestory lighting system must have existed in the western room.

The most difficult problem in trying to visualize the elevations of the various components of the Meeting Hall is to understand how the flanks were coordinated and how their roofing systems related to one another. The western, southern, and eastern flanks could have had been constructed with two stories even though these flanks were not as imposing as the northern. We must ask how their roofing systems were constructed. It seems unlikely that the roofs of the four flanks butted against each other. We have not found a single tile in the entire mass of architectural terracottas during twenty-one years of excavation which was made or cut to fit the line resulting from the intersection of two tile roofs of equal height at right angles. Thus the ridgepoles of the four flanks did not rise to the same height and were not in the same plane. The solution which seems most acceptable is one which allows the ridgepoles of the four roofs to be at different heights. Let me put forth one possibility. The peak of the northern flank's roof is the highest of the four and its ridgepole runs the entire length of the flank. The roofs of the western and eastern flanks rose to the same height, and their ridgepoles were slightly less than 50 m. in length because those roofs butted against the higher walls of the northern flank. Therefore, the eaves of the roof of the northern flank were above and extended over the roofs of the western and eastern flanks. The ridgepole of the southern flank was the lowest of the series and the shortest since it ran between the inner walls of the western and eastern flanks, or about 44 m. That roof butted against the higher walls of the western and eastern flanks, and the eaves of those roofs extended above it in the same way as the northern flank's roof extended over the roofs of the western and eastern flanks.

The three porches were also covered by roofs which butted against the exterior faces of the inner walls of the northern, eastern, and southern flanks. These roofs need not have had a steep slope but their upper edges, butting against the walls of the flanks, would have been protected by the overhang of the wide eaves of the northern, southern, and eastern flanks. The width of the intercolumniation in front of the eastern entrance is not too great for a single architrave, hence the roof of the eastern flank's porch could have covered that space. The three porches formed a continuous walkway around three sides of the central court.

THE TERRACOTTA REVETMENTS OF THE ARCHAIC MEETING HALL

The architectural revetments of the Archaic Meeting Hall, which I have dated on stylistic grounds and on the evidence of imported pottery to the early sixth century B.C.,[39] make up a complete system. They are among the earliest known Archaic Etruscan examples. Although they may be separated into two groups, namely those modeled by hand and those which were mold-made, all are from local clay and were made at Poggio Civitate.[40] Furthermore, the mold-made terracottas are so similar in technique and style that they were made in the same local workshop. The human and animal statues, as well as the feline spouts of the lateral simas which were modeled by hand, form a clear stylistic unit. These terracottas were part of the original building phase of the Archaic Meeting Hall. A very few pieces may have been damaged and replaced at a later

FIGURE 9:
Akroterion. Seated statue, r. side. Inv. 68–200 and 67–411. Max. restored Height, 1.70 m.

FIGURE 10:
Akroterion. Seated statue, front. Inv. 68–200 and 67–411.

FIGURE 11:
Akroterion. Seated statue, detail of the head. Inv. 68–200.

FIGURE 12:
Akroterion. Seated statue, detail of the hands. Inv. 67–411.

FIGURE 13:
Akroterion. Conservation and reconstruction of Inv. 67–411.

date; however, no archaeological evidence points to a mass replacement of revetments or indicates that the various types were made at different times. It is rare to have so many complete examples of architectural terracottas associated with a specific building whose broad features, plan, and elevation are known.

All sloping roofs were covered by pan and cover tiles. The normal pan tile of the Archaic building measures 0.63 m. in length and around 0.54 m. in width.[41] These tiles have flanges on their long sides and two rectangular notches at one end. These notches allowed the tile next in line to lock into place. When the pan tiles were placed on the roof, a crack remained between their flanges. This was covered by a cover tile whose width diminished toward its upper end so that it could easily slip under the tile next up the roof. The mass of the architectural terracottas at Poggio Civitate are these cover and pan tiles. In a real sense, they are the foundation of the entire revetment system, and most of the other architectural terracottas are developed from them and use the same unit of measurement, the Italic/Oscan foot of 0.27 m.

Archaic Terracotta Akroteria

It is easier to visualize the revetments of the roofing system if one starts at the ridgepole and works down the roof. The northern flank of the Archaic Meeting Hall was not only the most imposing but evidence for its decoration is more complete than for the other flanks. Its ridgepole was protected by a series of large tiles of varying lengths, yet the cross-section of each tile associated with this ridgepole is the same size and is nearly semicircular.

The Human Figures. A series of life-sized human figures, both seated and standing, and a number of real and fantastic animals were positioned along the length of the ridgepole. All the seated figures are placed perpendicular to the long axis of the tile on which they rest, while the standing humans and animals were in line with the axis of their tiles.

The most famous of these statues is a seated male wearing a broad-brimmed, high-peaked hat, often called "il cowboy." Two related fragments of similar material and scale were thought to be from the same statue and were displayed in Florence and Siena in 1970 as if from the same figure (Figs. 9–13: head and torso, Inv. 68–200; lower body, Inv. 67–411).[42] That reconstruction is from pieces now known to come from two different statues because the left side from shoulder to hip of Inv. 67–411 has been found. Although it is now clear that the fragments do not belong to the same piece, it is a correct visual image of the type. I therefore retain the composite for illustrative purposes. The figure's beard and hair, which falls down his back, have straight sides and a flat bottom. His lips are fleshy, and the eyes, rounded and full, are echoed by firmly rounded brows (Fig. 11). He sits on a four-legged stool, his forearms resting on his knees; his hands are held in a position to clasp a tubular object, such as a staff (Figs. 9 and 12). Note that the left thumb is up and the right down. The object held firmly in his hands may have identified him either as human or divine. (Other statues [Inv. 66–297[43] and Inv. 80–104[44]] held attributes clutched vertically in both hands, as do the figures on one of the frieze plaques [Fig. 53]). He wears a long garment terminating at the ankles and pointed shoes. His feet are on a footrest similar to examples depicted on the seated figures frieze (Fig. 52–54).

The statue was constructed in pieces and is hollow. A large passage runs from the ankles to the upper torso where small triangular openings, just under the armpits, pierce the body. All the seated statues were constructed in this manner and fired as one piece. (The hollow passage of Inv. 66–297 is well illustrated.)[45] Raffaele Del Corso, who restored the

sculpture, pointed out that this sophisticated system ensured that the statue's interior would have remained dry. The sun's rays would have warmed up the body cavity; the warm air in the cavity would have risen and exited through the triangular holes under the arms. At the same time fresh air would have been sucked into the statue, through the passage rising behind the lower skirt, drying out the interior of the statue.

The statue rests on a small portion of the ridgepole tile. An astounding feature of the seated statues is a tube which forms part of its structure. A hole, the size of the tube's hollow center, was cut into the ridgepole tile so that the tube could be attached to the tile, leaving a hole through the tile. Once the tube was in place, the four legs and upper portion of the stool's seat were affixed to it, thus forming the stool and effectively masking the tube which rises to the level of the top of the stool. The function of this tube is ingenious. A statue of the size and height of these would have created resistance to the wind, and a high wind could have toppled it from the roof had it not been firmly anchored. Its weight alone would not have been sufficient to ensure that it would not be blown down in a storm. Therefore, a sturdy, rounded beam was sunk into the ridgepole beam. This round beam, in reality a large dowel, was cut so that it filled the tube and reached to its top. The statue was slipped onto this large wooden dowel so that its base, the ridge-pole tile, sat on the ridgepole. In this manner, the statue was held in place and could not be thrown down by the elements. Other ridgepole figures, standing humans and animals, either preserve such tubes or the holes in the tiles around which they were fitted.

The figure with wide-brimmed, high-pointed hat is not the only type of seated figure. Another male[46] wears a close-fitting cap or helmet which has a pierced topknot (Fig. 14). Note the similarity of style between this head and the man with the peaked hat (Figs. 9–13), especially the form and modeling of the large eyes and the smoothing marks on the cheeks and forehead. The rudimentarily modeled ear, formed separately and then attached to the head, is a standard form on the Murlo statues. A large fragment from a statue preserves one breast and the scar for the second (Inv. 67–425),[47] indicating that akroteria in the form of seated or standing women also adorned the roof of the Archaic Meeting Hall's northern flank.

The exact number of seated figures which adorned the roof of the northern flank is difficult to calculate; however, according to Edlund-Berry's preliminary estimation,[48] more than thirteen existed. One particularly interesting example[49] preserves the lower portion of a figure's skirt and two well-shod feet resting on a footrest (Fig. 15). This is one of the few architectural terracottas from the site which preserves paint. The reddish brown skirt is bordered above the hem by two wide cream-colored bands, separated by a thin reddish brown strip. At the top of the upper band is a brown running key pattern. The garment was probably woven from wool. The creamy white is the natural color of wool, and the reddish brown may have been made from a natural bark dye. The pointed shoes or slippers were also two-toned. Their tops are reddish brown, and their sides and bottoms are creamy white, matching the tones of the skirt. Long creamy white laces tied these slippers, or soft shoes, which may also have been made from heavy wool.

Standing and walking human figures are less numerous than seated ones. A good example,[50] however, is preserved by the trailing foot of a walking figure shod in a pointed shoe (Fig. 16). The tube which supported this striding figure broke away from the ridgepole tile leaving only its scar and the hole which had been cut to receive its supporting dowel. A second tile preserves the forward foot of another striding figure (Inv. 71–330).[51] At first I identified a running figure, which is of much smaller scale than most of the human figures, as a Gorgon (Inv. 69–229),[52] but another running foot of nearly life-size proportions (Inv. 70–177)[53] suggests that both are simply running human figures. I doubt that the smaller running figures decorated the ridgepole

FIGURE 14:
Akroterion.
Seated statue
(?), helmeted
head, r. side.
Inv. 69–200.
Pres. Height,
0.23 m.

FIGURE 15:
Akroterion. Seated
statue, r. side.
Inv. 71–307.
Pres. Height of
garment, 0.34 m.

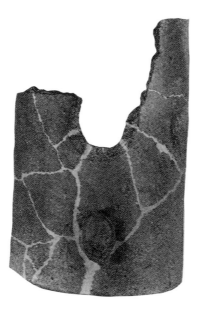

FIGURE 16:
Akroterion. Striding
figure, tile and shod
foot. Inv. 69–278.
Pres. Length, 0.58 m.

of the northern flank, but they could have been on one of the remaining three flanks.

Fantastic And Real Animals. The best-known fantastic animal from the site[54] is a standing male sphinx (Fig. 17), about the size of an Afghan hound. Fortunately a scrap of the ridgepole tile, the top edge just in front of the paired forepaws remains, so there is no doubt whatsoever that he is a ridgepole figure. The locks swooping down to the shoulders and the sharp outline of the wings, carried into and down the breast of the animal, are distinctive features; however, the creature's eyes, ears, and modeled mouth tie him firmly to the "Murlo style" as defined by Edlund-Berry. Fragments of other sphinxes have been found and these include at least one head (Inv. 68–635)[55] as well as other body parts.

Edlund-Berry[56] tentatively identifies one of the most fascinating heads from the site as that of another sphinx (Figs. 18 and 19). When I published the piece,[57] I suggested, because of its unusual style, that it was a replacement for an akroterion which had somehow been destroyed while the Meeting Hall was still in use.[58] I am less convinced now about my original dating of the head and wonder if it does not date from the building's original construction. I accept Edlund-Berry's identification of the head as that of a sphinx. The head, perhaps because of its greater elaboration, stands out as a major piece for understanding the Murlo hand-modeled terracotta production and the relationship of the Murlo school of sculpture to that of Chiusi.

Scheme of Akroteria. This host of akroteria in the form of seated, standing, striding, and running human figures in company with the fantastic animals would have stood out against the sky as a rich cresting, a fitting culmination for the architectural decoration of the Meeting Hall's northern flank. The seated figures, precisely because they would have been seen straight on, were the most important members of the sculptural group. Their companions, animals and other figures in human form, flanked them and accented their importance.

These seated male and female figures are difficult to interpret. Those who have identified them as ancestors or even magistrates have not considered the number and variety of akroteria on the ridgepole. Interpretations of the seated figures must take into account their accompanying host of human and fantastic figures. Standing figures in the presence of the seated figures brings to mind frieze plaques from Velletri on which the hero Herakles calmly stands in presence of seated gods.[59] I think a related scheme occurs on the ridgepole at Murlo where humans stand in respect for the seated divine figures. At Murlo the addition of heraldic fantastic animals, as one fre-

FIGURE 20:
Akroterion. Ram's head, r. side.
Inv. 68–280. Pres. Length,
0.14 m.

FIGURE 21:
Akroterion. Horse's head, r. side.
Inv. 66–259. Pres. Height, 0.18 m.

FIGURE 22:
Akroterion. Horse's head,
front. Inv. 66–259.

FIGURE 23:
Akroterion. Horse's head, l. side. Inv. 70–313.
Pres. Length, 0.24 m.

FIGURE 24:
Akroterion. Feline's leg, l.
side. Inv. 68–172.
Pres. Height, 0.19 m.

FIGURE 25:
Akroterion. Feline's
leg. front. Inv.
68–172.

and how to fire them once constructed. The ancestors of these figured akroteria mounted on ridgepoles are to be found in the pre-Archaic, Orientalizing period at Poggio Civitate (see below), Acquarossa, Tuscania, and Rome. The use of such members continues throughout the history of Etruscan architecture as manifested by an especially important set of Late Archaic akroteria from Veii.

Archaic Terminal Tiles and Plaques

The second large group of architectural terracottas, all made from the same local clay and drawn from molds, are pieces for protecting certain wooden members of the Archaic buildings from the elements. With one exception they covered the ends or the sides of exposed beams. The molds from which the terracottas were drawn were made at the same time and probably in the same workshop. It is possible that they were brought to the site or that they circulated from one site to another, just as the matrix used to make the molds for frieze plaques were shared by craftsmen at Rome, Veii, and Velletri.[69] The entire system hangs together as a unified artistic and constructional unit. Proof for this rests in the fact that the frieze plaques, lateral and raking simas, and pan tiles are all 0.54 ± m. wide (equivalent to two local feet). The secondary features of the frieze plaques—the studs and guilloche—are the same on the four types. Furthermore, the moldings on the frieze plaques are identical and are closely related to those of the lateral and raking simas.[70] The style of the reliefs on the frieze plaques and the raking sima is so close that their molds could have been made by the same man; he also may have made the molds for the Gorgon and feline plaques.

Gorgoneia Antefixes. It is impossible to know where and how all the molded revetments were placed on the wooden superstructure of the Archaic Meeting Hall. Even though the location of many may be postulated, only those decorated with Gorgoneia can be placed with certainty. A series of antefix plaques displaying the Gorgon's severed head were discovered in the destruction debris lying to the north of the Archaic Meeting Hall's northern flank by Erik Nielsen and Jenifer Neils. They were found about 0.5–0.6 m. apart, in a line from 7–8 m. to the north of the flank's foundation, lying parallel to the outside of the Meeting Hall's northern side. The line of antefixes therefore ran the entire length of the building. We

FIGURE 27:
Gorgoneion tile
with antefix
plaque. Inv.
72–235. Length
of tile, 0.60 m.

FIGURE 26:
Gorgoneion. Antefix
plaque. Inv.
68–68.
Height, 0.16 m.

FIGURE 28:
Tiles with antefix plaques in position on restored Archaic Meeting
Hall in the Palazzo Publico in Siena.

FIGURE 29:
Gorgoneion. Small
antepagmentum.
Inv. 67–10. Pres.
Height, 0.12 m.

FIGURE 30:
Gorgoneion. Large
antepagmentum.
Inv. 68–220. Pres.
Height, 0.24 m.

FIGURE 31:
Antepagmenta *and antefix plaques on restored Archaic Meeting*
Hall in the Palazzo Publico in Siena.

assume that they revetted the lower edge of the roof and fell in place where they were found when the northern wall of the complex was pushed over. The total number of Gorgoneia so far excavated is more than would have been required for the eaves of the exterior of the northern flank; consequently, it is thought that they also terminated the eaves of the portion of the northern flank's roof which jutted over the northern porch of the courtyard.

The Gorgoneia descended from a common ancestor and are extant in a series of different generations drawn from molds which make up a tight sequence.[71] A nearly perfectly preserved example[72] and another, one of the very few attached to its complete cover tile backer,[73] illustrate the type and its function (Figs. 26 and 27). The bulging eyes, trilobed nose, tooth-filled mouth, and lolling tongue are prominent features. The ears give the impression of being an afterthought; their outline, however, is similar to those of the seated statue. Traces of red color on the faces of a few Gorgoneia prove that they were originally painted. The Gorgoneion, in reality a shield to keep wind from blowing up the line of cover tiles, was attached to the tile so that its vertical face was not straight up and down; rather, its lower edge was drawn back toward the rear of the tile (Fig. 28). In this way, the plaque hooked under, ever so slightly, the edge of the roof and helped hold the tile in place. A second modification of the tile backer is the flange at its far end, which fitted securely under the next tile up the roof, again assuring that the tile remained in place in a high wind. Only the terminal tiles with the Gorgoneia plaques seem to have this flange.

Two specialized Gorgoneia, which are *antepagmenta,* or protective plaques, have been excavated. One, drawn from the same mold as the others in the series, has a smooth back and is pierced by a nail hole (Fig. 29).[74] This piece probably covered the end of one of the long wooden beams running the length of the roof of the northern flank. The second *antepagmentum,* hand-modeled, is much larger (Fig. 30) and is one of the two needed to protect the ends of the ridgepole of the Meeting Hall's northern flank (Fig. 31).[75] Its restored width is slightly larger than the standard width of the ridgepole tiles on which the seated statues sat.

The meaning of the Gorgon antefixes and *antepagmenta* of Poggio Civitate was probably identical to that of similar architectural pieces from Greece, South Italy, and Sicily. In other words, in addition to functioning as protection against the elements for certain wooden members of the building's roof, these mythical monsters were also intended to keep away evil and misfortune from the buildings they adorned.

Raking Sima. The raking sima may be illustrated by one example, complete except for a portion of its strigilated crown and its backer (Fig. 32).[76] Its fascia is decorated by two hounds in full pursuit of two hares (Fig. 33), a lively hunt frequently depicted on Protocorinthian and East Greek pottery of the late Orientalizing period. The spirited nature of the chase is appreciated when three of the raking simas are mounted in line, as they were in the display formerly housed in the Palazzo Comunale of Siena (see below, Fig. 56).[77] The animals rush left with extended strides, as represented by the hares (Fig. 34).[78]

Unfortunately, we cannot establish exactly how these terminal tiles were attached to the roof, even though we think they decorated the edges of certain gables of the Archaic Meeting Hall. There are many fewer raking than lateral simas, and I wonder if they were not restricted to the gables of the northern flank. Françoise-Hélène Massa-Pairault, who is publishing these pieces, has found one fragment which turns the angle of the roof. If this member revetted only the northern flank, only four such specialized tiles would have been needed for the entire complex, and we are lucky to have found one of them. The piece proves that lateral and raking simas were not used on the same slanting roof because the height of their fascias and crowns differs. The raking sima could, however, have revetted the gable of a roof whose eaves terminated in antefixes (in the form of Gorgoneia, as discussed above).

Before turning to the problems of the lateral sima, let me briefly summarize how the roof of the northern flank appeared when first erected. Its decorative revetments, those discussed above, are virtually certain. Statues crested its ridgepole; raking simas with hounds chasing hares edged its gables; Gorgoneia, decorating the ends of the cover tiles at the edges of the roof, accented its eaves at even intervals; and *antepagmenta,* also in the form of Gorgoneia, protected the ends of its mutules and ridgepole.

Lateral Sima. The largest molded revetment, and the single most common one from the Archaic Complex, is the heavy lateral sima.[79] Even though the following discussion is complex, I have decided to include it here because the lateral sima is one of our most important revetments for understanding the terracotta production at Poggio Civitate and the roofing system of the Archaic Meeting Hall. A series of fragments have been reconstructed to explain the form of this complicated revetment (Fig. 35). The fascia, strigilated cavetto, and backer of the sima were molded in one piece. A well-preserved example gives the height and width of the sima, part of the feline spout, and most of the attached Daedalic head (Figs. 36 and 37).[80] After the sima was removed from its mold, a hole was cut in the fascia and a hand-molded feline spout was inserted. The feline's ears were made separately and added at the back of the

FIGURE 35:
*Detail of
reconstruction of the
lateral sima in the
Palazzo Publico in
Siena*

FIGURE 36:
*Lateral sima, fascia.
Inv. no. 68–120.
Length, 0.54 m.*

FIGURE 37:
*Lateral sima,
Daedalic head.
Inv. no. 67–20.
Pres. Height,
0.13 m.*

FIGURE 38:
Lateral sima, fr. with feline spout, front view. Inv. 68–178. Height of spout, 0.10 m.

FIGURE 39:
Lateral sima, fr. with feline spout, top view. Inv. 68–178.

FIGURE 40:
Lateral sima, Daedalic head, front view. Inv. 68–152. Height, 0.11 m.

FIGURE 41:
Lateral sima, Daedalic head, front view. Inv. 68–504. Height, 0.21 m.

FIGURE 42:
Lateral sima, fr. of underside of backer. Inv. 71–170. Pres. Length, 0.18 m.

down the roof during a rainstorm. The water, before passing through the feline spout, could have filled this space and flowed over the edges of the sima-backer. The weight of the water would have added to the instability of the sima and might even have dislodged it from the roof's eaves. If, on the other hand, the bottom of the lateral sima were nearly parallel to the ground, its tile-backer, with its high flanged sides, would have formed a catch basin measuring about 0.49 x 0.7 x 0.60 (?) m. This basin could have contained the rain water descending from the sloping roof and channeled it through the feline waterspouts in an even flow. The water would have been distributed throughout the catch basin so that no extra strain would have been placed on the system used to hold the sima in place, and the water would have been directed away from the roof.[90]

I am fully aware that the section of the roof whose eaves were revetted with this sima was unusual. The tiles of the slanting portion of the roof, both pan and cover, would have terminated in a line so that the tile-backer of the sima would have fitted under them. The lower edge of the sloping roof's pan tiles may have been only a few centimeters above the upper surface of the cover tiles which must have covered the crack formed when the flanges of the two horizontal simas were placed side by side.

I think the lateral simas terminated the roofing system of the porches which surrounded three sides of the Meeting Hall's central court. Fragments of simas have been discovered over the entire site, which would be expected if they originally edged a number of the Meeting Hall's roofs. We know that at least 206 simas, as represented by Daedalic heads and scars for such heads, adorned the building. These simas are enough to accommodate 112 m. of roof, which, however, is less than would have been required to edge the eaves of the three porches of the court. The simas, resting on the wooden beams running the length of the porches, above their wooden columns or pilasters, were securely fixed in place so that their decorated underside made up the first level of the roof's painted ornament. The feline spouts, rosettes, and Daedalic heads formed a decorative band running around the entire court, defining its edges (Fig. 43). The feline spouts, placed far from the earthen walkways of the porches, ensured that the floors of the porches were dry even during the wet days of fall, winter, and spring.

A small group of Ionic heads which adorned the right edge of certain lateral simas have also been found (Fig. 44).[91] The fragment could have been introduced as a replacement if one of the original lateral simas, decorated with a

FIGURE 43:
Reconstruc-
tion of the
lateral sima
in the
Palazzo
Publico in
Siena.

FIGURE 43:
Reconstruc-
tion of the
lateral sima
in the
Palazzo
Publico in
Siena.

FIGURE 44:
Lateral sima, fr. with
Ionic head. Inv.
68–195. Pres.
Height, 0.17 m.

FIGURE 45:
Mold for
Daedalic head,
front view.
Inv. 70–129.
Pres. Height,
0.17 m.

Daedalic head, had been damaged. I think, although I cannot prove it, that the Ionic heads are stylistically later than the Daedalic. Perhaps these simas were part of the repairs carried out when the eastern section of the northern flanks's exterior wall gave way.[92]

As stated above, the lateral simas, with their fascias, cavettos, and backers, were drawn from complex molds. The rosettes and Daedalic heads were made from other molds and then attached. Fortunately, we found one fragmentary mold of a Daedalic head used at the site (Fig. 45).[93] The mold is made of a fine-grained terracotta, carefully smoothed on its inner side so that the impression is without blemishes. The back of the mold is rounded so that it would easily fit into the workman's hands. This mold proves that the terracottas which adorned the Archaic Meeting Hall were made and fired at the site. Naturally, the mold could have been taken from an object brought to Murlo, perhaps a metal head, by a wandering craftsman who later took his models elsewhere. The value of this piece for understanding the craft of architectural terracottas at Poggio Civitate cannot be overestimated.

Fragments of raking and lateral simas are very common in the debris associated with the destruction of the Archaic Building Complex (Fig. 46). Complete examples of both members have been put together. Both are 0.54 m. wide and crowned by a strigilated molding; obviously they are from the same roofing system and are terminal tiles that protected the edges of the wooden roofs. The strigils of both simas are closely related to those on the frieze plaques; furthermore, the guilloche bordering the lower edge of the raking sima's fascia is identical to those on the frieze plaques. Therefore, the three members from Poggio Civitate—raking simas, lateral simas, and frieze plaques—are part of the same revetment system. Lucy Shoe Meritt thinks that this coordinated system of terminal tiles and frieze plaques could date as early as 600 B.C., and that it is the northern counterpart of the well-known examples from Poggio Buco and the Roman Forum.[94]

Frieze Plaques. Annette Rathje is studying the frieze plaques; each piece is being examined in order to establish its mold sequence and its construction. She has already formulated tentative interpretations of the scenes depicted[95] and will incorporate her ideas in an overall explanation of the Archaic Meeting Hall's architectural program. All the frieze plaques are the same in size, thickness, and form. All have similar cavetto crowns, rectangular studs above the picture field, a fascia decorated with a figural scene, and a running guilloche which serves as a ground line for the scene. Their width of 0.54 m. coordinates with the other revetments used on the Archaic buildings of Poggio Civitate. Furthermore, the strigi-

FIGURE 46:
Lateral sima with Daedalic head as found.

FIGURE 47:
Horse race and banquet frieze plaques as found to the SE
of the Archaic Meeting Hall, excavated by Erik O. Nielsen.

lated cavetto relates them to the lateral and raking simas, and the guilloche running along the lower border ties them to the raking simas. The hounds chasing hares on the raking sima resemble the dogs on the banquet frieze plaques. The four scenes are so close in style that the matrices from which their molds were drawn must have been made by the same craftsman. This is not the place to make a detailed stylistic analysis of the four types; however, all are Etruscan and all show strong influence from either Greece or South Italy of the late Orientalizing period. If our craftsmen were influenced by pieces made in Corinth, we could identify Protocorinthian pottery as the source for the influences; if influenced by objects from South Italy, we might look more closely to bronzes made at Taranto or Metaponto. The details of craftsmanship that can be seen in the best-preserved examples indicate the high artistic level of the northern artist who was responsible for making these low reliefs.

The four types are by now well known. Fortunately, examples of the banquet and horse race friezes, along with raking simas, were discovered as they had fallen at the southeast corner of the Archaic Meeting Hall (Fig. 47). They are among the very few architectural terracottas from the Archaic complex which were not carried away and buried ceremonially when the complex was deliberately destroyed. This debris layer proves that the lateral simas, their related raking simas, and the frieze plaques were part of the same decorative period which has been dated between 600 and 590 B.C. A quick review of the four types will bring them into focus.

The *banquet frieze* is marvelously precise and balanced in its organization (Fig. 48).[96] Penny Small, in her basic study, explains its Etruscan nature and its relationship to Greek art.[97] The furniture,[98] musical instruments, vases, bedding, and food depicted in this scene are valuable documents for understanding an early Etruscan symposium. Wine, food, music, and conversation were shared by well-attended couples who leisurely enjoyed their surroundings. Details of the relief are unusually fine; for example, the handles of wine pitchers and drinking cups are sharp and crisp. Carefully profiled faces, delicately formed hands, and precisely arranged hair styles document the elegance of the banquet. Very early stylistic traits mark the low relief. Note how the arms of the second reclining figure from the left and of the second serving figure cut back into the body of the second figure. The *lebes,* at the center of the composition, even more obviously invades the two servants standing behind it (Fig. 49). Three features may indicate that the artist who created the patrix for the banquet frieze's mold was copying an early low relief, perhaps in metal. The chest of the first figure reclining at the left

FIGURE 48:
Banquet frieze.
Inv. 69–220.
Length, 0.55 m.

FIGURE 49:
Banquet frieze.
Detail of lebes or
cauldron.

FIGURE 50:
Horse race frieze.
Inv. 72–230.

is missing, and his right lower arm and wrist were mistaken for the handle of a vase. This mistake is particularly important because vases in the shape of legs, etc., are frequent in Late Orientalizing Etruscan bucchero, and the Etruscan artist was reproducing what he thought he saw in his model. Probably this figure was waving to his companion with his left hand. The third mistake is another omission: the leftmost dog has no rear right leg. One wonders if the craftsman who made the patrix was adapting a Greek relief of the late seventh century B.C. or working from a design on an Early Corinthian krater.

The second frieze type is a *horse race* (Fig. 50). Three horses and their riders rush right in a spirited race. The *lebes* sitting on an Etruscan column may be a trophy, if one reads each frieze plaque as an independent unit; however, if the entire series of plaques forms a sequence, the repeating columns crowned by metal pots would be guideposts. As Lucy Shoe Meritt points out, the molding at the base of the column and the capital with its hawksbeak are Etruscan forms,[99] and Margaret Root aptly writes that "when all the stylistic and representational qualities of the figural decoration on the horse race frieze are drawn together they describe a scene which is decidedly Etruscan, though heavily influenced by Protocorinthian and Corinthian vase painting traditions."[100]

I think it important that the banquet and horse race frieze plaques were found in an undisturbed destruction layer. There can be no doubt that the two types were associated with one another on the building. This association of banquet and horse race, which also occurs on Corinthian pottery and in Etruscan tombs at Chiusi, is a logical juxtaposition. Both scenes depict events which were enjoyed during times of leisure and festivity. We must, however, keep in mind that both games and banquets are also associated with heroic funerals.

Perhaps because of their greater emphasis on seated and standing draped human figures, the remaining two frieze types, a *procession* and *an assembly of seated figures with their attendants,* seem to form a coordinated pair, just as do the banquet and horse race scenes. The fragments of these friezes were found scattered over the entire site. The less common is the procession frieze,[101] which is preserved in one complete example (Fig. 51)[102] and a number of fragments, one of which is an excellent impression of the figures seated on their cart.[103] Although this procession is rendered precisely, its meaning is difficult to establish. Two attendants lead two horses drawing a two-wheeled cart on which sits a couple under an umbrella. Attendants, carrying gifts (fans, small situlas, a covered pot, and a stool), follow.[104] Timothy Gantz thinks the procession depicts a series of noblemen approaching the gods on the seated figures frieze (Fig. 52); Emanuela Fabricotti compares the frieze with examples from Serra di Vaglio, Metaponto, and S. Biagio, thus introducing the possibility that the procession may depict either a human or a sacred wedding.[105] I wonder about the relationship of the frieze with funerals because of its parallels with stelae now in the Civic Museum in Bologna.[106] Combinations of these ideas may interpret the frieze; however, we should keep in mind that processions in which highly placed persons are drawn along seated on wagons or carts may have special meanings in antiquity. We need only recall the advent of Tarquin and Tanaquil into Rome, and the ruse by which one of the Peisistratids regained power in Athens by dressing up a large Athenian girl as Athena and riding with her up to the Acropolis. This frieze remains one of the finest examples of Murlo craftsmanship.

The final frieze type, *seated figures*,[107] illustrated here by one restored example (Fig. 52), is an amazing combination of figures and their possessions.[108] Men and women, both seated and standing, face right. The seated figures, each holding an object or attribute, sit on stools, with the exception of one who is honored with a high-backed throne. All rest their feet on stools. The first male has an attendant who holds his sword and spear. The first seated female is served by a woman holding her fan and small situla.

The following three seated figures are guarded by a man holding a large staff. Gantz interpreted the figures as divine,[109] arguing that the first group represents the Capitoline Triad of Jupiter, Minerva, and Juno (Fig. 53), and that the second group is the Aventine Triad of Persephone, Dionysus, and Demeter (Fig. 54). His attributions have been contested; however, I accept those of Jupiter, Juno, Persephone, Dionysus, and Demeter and believe that all the figures are gods, even the serving man and woman. Others identify the figures as officials or magistrates at games,[110] or members of the family which owned Poggio Civitate,[111] or an assembly of gods.[112] The details of the frieze are exceedingly fine and it will remain one of the central subjects for discussion and interpretation for many years.

The four scenes of the frieze plaques form an artistic and iconographic unit. Obviously whoever built the Archaic Meeting Hall on Poggio Civitate selected them for a precise reason, even though we may never fully understand that reasoning. The very large number of fragments of the four types, and their scattered distribution on the site, makes it impossible to know where they went on the Archaic Meeting Hall. They could have covered the wooden architraves of the three porches within the court, thus providing a lively series of scenes banding the court itself. They also could have revetted the wooden beams which capped the wooden

FIGURE 51:
Procession frieze.
Inv. 69–384.
Length, 0.54 m.

FIGURE 52:
Seated figures
frieze. Inv.
68–264.
Length, 0.54 m.

FIGURE 53:
Detail of seated figures frieze. Inv. 68–309.
Height, 0.23 m.

FIGURE 54:
Detail of seated figures frieze. Inv. 68–313.
Height, 0.23 m.

pilasters supporting the earthen walls of the northern flank. In that position they would have been high above their viewers, in a dark room. I wonder if they might not have been organized in tiers, perhaps on the outer earthen walls under the roofs of the porches, in a manner similar to painted friezes which circle Proto-corinthian and Corinthian pottery. They may also have been organized in groups of alternating scenes, for example banquet-horse race-banquet, or seated figures-procession-seated figures. For purposes of this present report, I defer interpretation of the four frieze plaques to Annette Rathje.

The final group of mold-made revetments associated with the Archaic Meeting Hall is a series of small leopard protomes.[113] All descend from a single patrix which probably was made at the end of the seventh century B.C. Just as with the Gorgon plaques and the Daedalic heads, a series of molds and a number of generations within each series exists. The

pieces, best represented by one intact head (Fig. 55),[114] have a wonderful balance of crisp lines and broadly modeled features. One example (Inv. 68–161) preserves a portion of the hooked backer and its nail hole.[115] The member was slipped over a wooden beam and then held in place by a nail. This revetment is the only one which cannot be understood as a specialized tile for protecting a particular wooden portion of the building from rain. I have postulated that these feline protomes were placed on the architraves which ran along the top of the wooden columns holding up the roof of the porch of the northern flank. They served no purpose other than as guardians of the crossing from the court into the northern flank.

A number of terracottas defy identification and date, yet they are related to the entire group known from the site. One particularly fine piece is a small fragmentary human head (Inv. 71–167)[116] and another is a large stand (Inv. 67–450).[117]

Summary

The intertwining system of architectural terracottas which revetted the Archaic Meeting Hall on Poggio Civitate must have been conceived, executed, and mounted on the buildings within a short period of time. Gorgon plaques, feline protomes (both waterspouts and leopard masks), and female heads all have apotropaic powers and can be understood as devices to ward off evil from the build-

FIGURE 55:
Leopard protome. Inv. 70–200. Height, 0.11 m.

FIGURE 56:
Restored Archaic Meeting Hall in the Palazzo Publico in Siena showing
antepagmenta, *lateral sima, and frieze plaques.*

ing or the precinct. I think the figures seated on the roof are divine beings. Fantastic animals and minor divinities or heroes flank them or walk into their presence. Divine figures are frequently depicted in the company of fantastic animals on Orientalizing pottery and bronze reliefs, and the introduction of Herakles into Olympus demonstrates how a hero may enter the abode of the gods. The frieze plaques, and perhaps also the raking sima, introduce human elements into the decorative program of the Archaic Meeting Hall. Banquets, horseraces, hunts, and slow-moving processions are all human experiences which would have been shared by those who came to Poggio Civitate. (One need go no farther than Siena to witness a horserace, the annual Palio, run on an exceedingly dangerous course. A race from Piano del Tesoro, along the spine of Poggio Civitate to Poggio Aguzzo and back would have been much safer than the Palio held in the Campo of Siena.) I believe the seated figures depicted on the frieze plaques are intended to evoke divine figures; they might, however, have been humans acting the parts of gods—a Roman or Etruscan general who took part in a triumph dressed as a god and was treated as such during the triumphal ceremony.

The delegate who came to Poggio Civitate would have understood the decorative system which united and accented the Archaic complex. One should men-tally approach the Meeting Hall with this delegate. From a distance he would have seen the ridgepole statues cresting the roofs even though he probably would not have been able to make out their identity. Drawing nearer, he could have observed the Gorgon antefixes along the eaves of the northern flank's roof, the raking sima with its hounds and hares edging the gables, and the *antepagmenta*, also in the gables, in the form of Gorgoneia protecting the ends of the exposed beams which supported the roof (Fig. 56). Entering the building complex, the visitor would have stood in the central court and glanced at the northern flank. His eyes would have moved up the columns, past the architrave protected by the leopard protomes, to the lateral simas with their feline waterspouts, rosettes, and female heads evenly spaced at the edge of the porch roof. Above was the high roof of the northern flank, edged with Gorgoneia. At the very top of this roof was a crest of human and animal forms. The visitor may now have gone into the porch of the northern flank where detailed frieze plaques could have decorated the wall.

Even today as modern visitors to Poggio Civitate, we know that we are in the presence of a monumental complex whose architectural form and decoration had profound meaning. As I have stated many times, the iconographical meaning of the revetment system must have alluded to what took place at the site, and the Etruscans who frequented Poggio Civitate surely understood this decorative program. Unfortunately, we have no literary sources which identify Poggio Civitate and have only its material remains as a guide for understanding its meaning.

CEREMONIAL DESTRUCTION OF THE ARCHAIC MEETING HALL

To this point I have discussed the Archaic complex on Poggio Civitate as it appeared while still in use. Its destruction also must be examined because this event is an extremely important key for understanding the fuller implications of this discovery. Already in 1970 I argued that the buildings on Poggio Civitate were ritually destroyed during the third quarter of the sixth century B.C.[118] That hypothesis now seems certain. The latest Greek pottery at the site, fragments of Laconian III cups by the Hunt Painter (attributed by Stibbe) dating to the period 550/530 B.C.,[119] provide an approximate destruction date of the Archaic Meeting Hall. The buildings were deliberately torn down, many to their foundations. The architectural revetments, broken when the buildings were leveled, were taken to various locations on the site, buried, and hidden from view. Certain

pieces were taken to the west and laid down in a specially constructed dump. They were scattered on bedrock, perhaps in an area previously quarried, and then covered by a layer of small stones and earth to a depth of nearly 2 m. Others were thrown into the *fossae* which bordered the western and northern sides of Piano del Tesoro; those ditches were then filled with rubble and stones. Still others were buried in small pockets in the bedrock on Piano del Tesoro itself. Joins between fragments of the same architectural terracotta have been made with pieces found on Piano del Tesoro, pieces from the *fossa* to the west of Piano del Tesoro, and pieces buried under 2 m. of rubble within the ancient dump farther to the west.

Once the buildings on Poggio Civitate were torn down and their decorative terracottas ritually buried, much as were the terracotta revetments of the Portonaccio Temple at Veii, the site was circled by an earthen mound, or *agger*. The mound constructed over the western flank of the destroyed Archaic Meeting Hall is the best preserved. It covered the entire width of the flank and was preserved in spots to a height of 4 m. At the northern and southern ends of the western flank the mound turned east and circled Piano del Tesoro where erosion has eaten much of it away. This ceremonial destruction of the site set it out of bounds and made it *sacer* forever.

I think that this tabu against the occupation of Poggio Civitate continued throughout late antiquity into the Middle Ages. The hill is an ideal location for a Medieval town. High up with a commanding view, it dominates the northern side of the Ombrone River. Furthermore, natural springs dot its summit, providing water even during the summer months. Yet no one returned to build a town on the site precisely because it had been set out of bounds. A memory of this early settlement survives in the name Poggio Civitate, traced by Bianchi Bandinelli in early sixteenth-century Church records, but associated with the site as early as the first records of a Medieval comune which once existed to the south of Poggio Civitate. The name Poggio Civitate—"The Inhabited Hill"—may have been applied to the site when its Etruscan name fell from local use. I suspect this renaming occurred in the early Medieval period, during the period of Longobard dominance in the area.

I have argued that the Archaic Meeting Hall was destroyed by the rulers of ancient Chiusi during that city's expansion and development, dated to the second half of the sixth century B.C.[120] Poggio Civitate must have been important during the late seventh and sixth centuries B.C. Had it been just the residence of a local family, the rulers of Chiusi would have merely carried them into captivity and burned their holdings. The time, effort, and costs involved in ritually destroying the site indicates that Chiusi feared whatever existed at Poggio Civitate and wanted to make absolutely certain that the site never rose again. Only a sanctuary or rival political center of special importance could have aroused such fear and hatred. Any object which identified the function or purpose of the damned site had to be put out of view. The revetments, the "flags" for identifying the function of the Meeting Hall, had to be carefully buried. Even if broken, these pieces were important and had to be ritually obliterated; only then could Poggio Civitate be returned to its earlier isolation, a wooded hill or grove used by local hunters and woodsmen.

Part II

—

Excavations in the Orientalizing Meeting Hall

Excavations

By the end of our fourth season of excavation a decision was reached to excavate under the earthen floor levels of the Archaic Meeting Hall with the hope of finding secure ceramic evidence for dating its construction and to examine more thoroughly its building techniques. As noted earlier, the results of the excavations on Piano Del Tesoro are reported as found. Ordinarily the Orientalizing occupation would be reported first, then the Archaic would follow. Our system of excavation encourages reporting the finds and occupation periods as we excavated them.

We accomplished our aims, documented the construction techniques of the Meeting Hall, and found enough securely dated pottery to place the construction of the Meeting Hall after 610 B.C., or at the transition from the Orientalizing period to the Archaic period. The excavations revealed the foundations of an earlier Orientalizing building, constructed sometime between 675 and 650 B.C., and destroyed by fire slightly before 610 B.C. Finds associated with this structure include luxury objects of stone, ivory, fine pottery, and metal as well as a complete selection of everyday household objects. These excavations give precious insights into life in Northern Etruria during the seventh century B.C.

Ingrid Edlund-Berry made the first thorough soundings through the floor levels of the Archaic complex during the 1970 season. Because a test trench had been made previously within the western flank, we decided to continue exploration under the floor levels in that area. In order to facilitate and to control the work, we limited excavations to those areas

FIGURE 57:
Bronze wrestlers and
umpire, as found.
Excavation photo.

FIGURE 58:
Bronze umpire. Inv.
71–106. Height,
0.06 m.

FIGURE 59:
Bronze wrestler.
Inv. 71–105.
Height, 0.09 m.

FIGURE 60:
Early Corinthian
skyphos. Inv. 71–393.
Height, 0.07 m.

bounded by the foundation walls of the Archaic building. A number of rectangles, defined by the foundation walls of the various rooms, established the scope of the excavations. We knew that the material lying under the floors of the Archaic building, within the foundation walls of its rooms, constituted a series of sealed deposits which could shed light on the construction date of the buildings on Piano del Tesoro.

The floor levels in the western flank were easy to distinguish. Their compact earthen surfaces, leveled and beaten in antiquity, varied between 0.05 and 0.10 m. in depth and were of a fine, yellowish texture. (Nearly all of these floors had been covered by layers of broken tiles and architectural terracottas which had been cleared during the first four years of excavations.) The bottom layer of the earthen floors was less fine and appeared darker and coarser. The initial excavation within the floor levels in Rectangle 6 (Fig. 61) did not prepare us for what was to come when work started the next year, 1971, in Rectangle 7. Within a heavily burned stratum, filled with large pieces of carbon, two small bronzes suddenly appeared (Fig. 57), an umpire (Fig. 58)[121] and two wrestlers (Fig. 59),[122] one of which is preserved only by his lower wrist. The two nearly complete figures, so heavily burned that they had started to melt, lack their feet. The three form a group, two wrestlers and their umpire, which must

have been attached to an elaborate bronze vessel. Only later, after we had discovered a large selection of Etruscan and Greek pottery in the same destruction layer, could we date these small Etruscan masterpieces. Because they were in context with an Early Corinthian skyphos (Fig. 60)[123] and a series of Ionic and Laconian II cups,[124] they had to have been made within the closing years of the seventh century B.C.

Before turning to other pieces found in the debris layers under the earthen floor levels of the Archaic Meeting Hall, a review of the archaeological context of the finds is necessary in order to understand their implications for the site. We quickly became aware that we were within the debris of an early set of buildings which burned sometime during the late seventh century B.C. The buildings probably caught fire and burned so quickly that the inhabitants did not have time to save the many precious pieces of pottery, bronze, ivory, and even gold and silver which were part of their holdings. (A similar violent destruction has been documented recently for workshops to the south of the Orientalizing and Archaic Meeting Halls).[125] The earthen walls of the earlier structure were pushed over and scattered about. Then trenches for the foundations of the Archaic Meeting Hall were dug through this debris, disturbing even more the pottery, architectural terracottas, and the household objects associated with the Orientalizing building. The find-spots of a series of fragmentary Ionic bowls from the floor levels of the Orientalizing Long Buildings and within the rubble stone foundations of the Archaic Meeting Hall[126] demonstrate how the material in the debris layers was smashed, scattered, and moved about during the building of the Archaic structures. Once the earthen floors of the Archaic Building were laid down, however, the objects under them were sealed within a series of small compartments or rectangles which remained unchanged or uncontaminated by other materials until we excavated.[127]

THE ORIENTALIZING MEETING HALL: DATE, PLAN, AND CONSTRUCTION

The earliest pottery within the occupation levels on Piano del Tesoro dates between 675 and 650 B.C.; thus it is probable that these Orientalizing buildings were standing before 650 B.C. The Orientalizing Long Building lies under portions of the western flank and the western side of the court of the Archaic Meeting Hall.[128] To the south, and at right angles to this Orientalizing Long Building, is a structure made up of a series of small rooms opening onto a porch with a colonnade (Fig. 61).[129] An open space, similar to that at Acquarossa,[130] is formed by the western and southern components of the Orientalizing Buildings. No remains of Orientalizing foundations have been found to the east or north of this open space. Those to the east, if they existed, would have been destroyed by later erosion as were most of the foundations of the Archaic complex in that area. In all probability the Archaic complex followed the general organization of the Orientalizing buildings. Both have an area defined by surrounding structures. This central area, surely a court in the Archaic Meeting Hall and probably one in the Orientalizing buildings, was flanked by porches.

Further to the south on Piano del Tesoro are a series of workshops whose exact chronology has yet to be established.[131] The small building to the north of the northern flank of the Archaic Meeting Hall may have been erected in

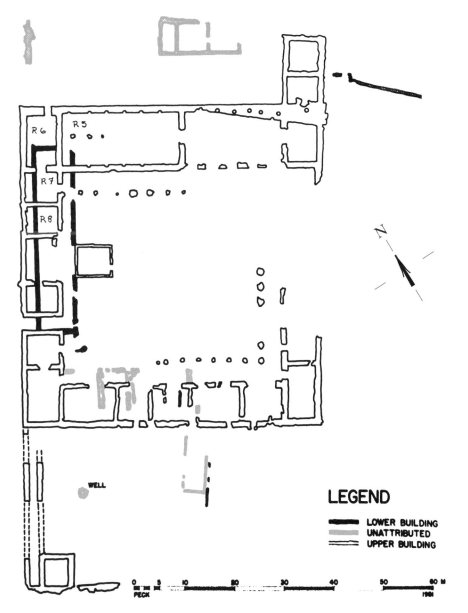

R6 R5

R7

R8

N

WELL

LEGEND

LOWER BUILDING
UNATTRIBUTED
UPPER BUILDING

0   5   10   20   30   40   50   60 M
PECK   1981

FIGURE 61:

Schematic plan of Orientalizing buildings on Piano del Tesoro.

the period between the destruction of the Orientalizing complex and the Archaic Meeting Hall because its orientation is the same as that of the northern flank.[132]

The construction techniques of the Orientalizing and Archaic Buildings are the same. Rubble foundations supported earthen walls which were coated with fine lime plaster. The floor levels, when preserved, are of beaten earth. The Orientalizing Long Building on the western side of Piano del Tesoro had at least two stories. The ground floor room was filled with large pithoi set into the earthen floor. In and around these storage jars was a heavy concentration of carbon from the burned wooden beams which had supported the second floor and its rooms. The household objects scattered about, both in and around the broken pithoi, indicate that they had fallen from an upper floor into the storage rooms when the structure burned. Tiles from the roof were found in various places, some more or less intact. Because no changes in building techniques, and very little in the orientation, can be detected in the buildings of the Orientalizing and Archaic periods on Piano del Tesoro, we assume that the people who lived in the Orientalizing complex built new quarters in the same location as soon as possible after their old ones burned.

Terracotta Revetments of the Orientalizing Meeting Hall

Fortunately, the parallels between the Orientalizing and Archaic buildings are not limited to orientation and general construction. The rich decorative assemblages of the Archaic Meeting Hall had their predecessors in a series of architectural terracottas, including pan and cover tiles, found in association with the Orientalizing Meeting Hall. The earlier pan and cover tiles are not as standardized as those of the Archaic Meeting Hall; however, Wikander establishes that they are precursors of the fully developed system employed by the craftsmen who constructed the roof of the later Archaic buildings.[133]

The Orientalizing architectural revetments are more difficult to associate with precise structures than the Archaic revetments; however, the find-spots of three (a complete ridgepole tile, a horse-and-rider akroterion, and fragments of the raking sima) tie some of them to the Orientalizing Long Building sealed under the floor levels of the Archaic Meeting Hall's western flank. The most complete is the ridgepole tile with its crowning voluted triangle,[134] which was sealed under the floor levels of Room 6 of the Archaic complex. Therefore, other voluted triangular elements (Fig. 62)[135] or cut-out spirals (Inv. 70–104),[136] many of which were found in more disturbed contexts, probably adorned buildings of the Orientalizing period on Piano del Tesoro. Nielsen publishes cut-out akroteria found in burned debris of the long southern stoa-like building which he excavated.[137]

Fragments of the horse-and-rider akroterion (Fig. 63)[138] were found in two spots, one outside the western wall of the Orientalizing Long Building and the other to the north of the Archaic Meeting Hall's northern flank. The piece broke when it fell from the roof during the fire which destroyed the Long Orientalizing Building. Its fragments were scattered when the area was leveled for the later Archaic buildings. This horse and rider is among our earliest figural akroteria and displays a very primitive form. The two-dimensional group is distinguished by its outlines; however, just as with many rock-cut door jambs from early tombs at Tarquinia, the interior details are deep grooves. Another primitive horse and rider, reconstructed from fragments by Rystedt, was found in a mixed context with the Orientalizing structures.[139] Since the first horse-and-rider akroterion can definitely be assigned to the Orientalizing Long Building, this second one also

belongs here. Only the rear quarters and the head are preserved (Figs. 64 and 65).[140] The outline of the horse is in sharp silhouette. Taken together these two horse-and-rider akroteria push back our knowledge of freestanding akroterial sculpture well into the seventh century B.C., a period which archaeologists call either early Etruscan or late Villanovan.

A third architectural member associated with the Orientalizing Long Building is the plain raking sima.[141] Two examples were in the destruction debris of the *agger*, on the earthen floor of the Archaic building's western flank. They may have been scraped up with the earth from the lower levels which was piled up to build the *agger* during the final destruction of the site. The pieces, identified by Wikander, have a backer and a high side flange fitted with a notch that could lock into a corresponding notch in an adjacent sima.[142] No decoration adorns the smooth fascia of the raking sima, nor does its fascia have a strigilated cavetto crown. The fascia, however, could have been painted in antiquity as were related pieces from Acquarossa.[143]

We do not know if the eaves of this Orientalizing Long Building were revetted with antefixes or with lateral simas.[144] Because a few fragments of these early simas were found in the dump to the west of the Archaic complex during the first years of excavation, they could have revetted the eaves of the Orientalizing Long

FIGURE 62:
*Orientalizing
ridgepole tile,
cresting in the form
of a cut-out voluted
triangle. Inv. 71–310.
Pres. Height, 0.36 m.*

FIGURE 66:
*Orientalizing
lateral sima, fr.
of water spout.
Inv. 66–229.
Height, 0.13 m.*

FIGURE 63:
*Orientalizing
ridgepole tile,
horse-and-rider
akroterion. Inv.
69–284. Pres.
Height, 0.32 m.*

FIGURE 67:
*Orientalizing fr.
of antefix, front
view.
Inv. 68–196.
Height, 0.13 m.*

FIGURE 64:
*Horse-and-rider
akroterion of the
Orientalizing period,
rear quarters of the
horse. Inv. 68–475.
Pres. Width, 0.21 m.*

FIGURE 68:
*Orientalizing fr.
of antefix, side
view.
Inv. 68–196.
Pres. Length of tile,
0.12 m.*

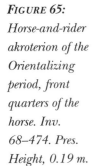

FIGURE 65:
*Horse-and-rider
akroterion of the
Orientalizing
period, front
quarters of the
horse. Inv.
68–474. Pres.
Height, 0.19 m.*

FIGURE 69:
*Orientalizing
terracotta
Griffin, smoke
tile (?). Side view.
Inv. 68–50. Pres.
Height, 0.21 m.*

Building, although most of them are associated with the stoa-like workshops to the south of the Archaic complex.[145] The lateral sima, like its Archaic descendant, has as its central feature a feline water-spout. The upper portion of the feline head of the earlier sima's water-spout was mold-made; its fangs and the lower jaw, however, were hand-made additions. A particularly good example of the mold-made portion of the spout was found during our first season (Fig. 66).[146] This spout was inserted within a hole cut in the smooth fascia of the sima; because the sima has no crowning cavetto, however, the feline head is higher than the upper border of the sima's fascia. At the upper right and left edges of the sima's smooth fascia are half-rounded notches positioned so that they are a few centimeters from one another when two simas are placed side by side.

In 1968 we found a particularly interesting, and stylistically early, antefix in the dump to the west of the Archaic complex (Figs. 67 and 68).[147] Since then Nielsen has excavated a large number of closely related heads, including the mold for one of the series, in the area to the south of the Archaic Meeting Hall.[148] He associates them with the early lateral simas and demonstrates that the sides of the antefixes slip precisely into the two rounded notches cut into the upper outer edges of the simas' fascias when two simas are placed side by side. The head hangs over the two simas and masks the crack between them just as its backer covers the crack between their contiguous flanges.[149] The applied Daedalic heads on the later Archaic lateral sima are a simplification of this earlier, more complex system.

Other Orientalizing architectural revetments are known and are being worked on for publication. I present one last fragment (Fig. 69), a problem piece because it is such a fine terracotta.[150] This large griffin's head was found in surface soil near the rectangular enclosure on the western side of the Archaic building's central court. Therefore, its context neither dates it nor ties it to a particular period at the site. Its features—wide-open mouth, "metallic" topknot, and curls at the side of the head—are fully Orientalizing and suggest a date within the seventh century B.C. Because it is hollow, I have postulated that it was part of a specialized tile,[151] similar to ones known from Acquarossa, which allowed smoke to escape through the roof of a closed room.[152]

The Orientalizing terracottas at Poggio Civitate form a unit. If, as I think, the Orientalizing Long Building sealed under the western flank of the Archaic Meeting Hall was standing by 650 B.C., these terracottas are among the very earliest known from the Etruscan world. Only certain pieces from Acquarossa may be of the same period.[153] The forms of the revetments from Murlo and Acquarossa are already set in the seventh century B.C.

FIGURE 70:
Local buccheroid bowl with
low conical foot, side view.
Inv. 71–80. Height, 0.06 m.

FIGURE 71:
Local bucchero kantharos with
flat ring base, profile view.
Inv. 71–71. Height, 0.11 m.

FIGURE 72:
Local bucchero kantharos with
low conical foot, profile view.
Inv. 73–212. Height, 0.13 m.

FIGURE 73:
Local bucchero
kyathos with low
conical foot and double
molded handle, slant view. Inv.
72–280. Height, 0. 19 m.

FIGURE 74:
Outside of handle with winged
female figure. Inv. 72–280.

FIGURE 75:
Inside of handle with molded
plaque. Inv. 72–280.

FIGURE 76:
Local bucchero kantharos with low conical foot, fluted body, and double molded handle. Side view. Inv. 73–239. Height, 0.16 m.

FIGURE 77:
Detail of outside of handle with molded female figure. Inv. 73–239.

FIGURE 78:
Detail of inside of handle with molded tree-of-life. Inv. 73–239.

FIGURE 79:
Fragmentary scalloped bowl, inside of the double handle. Inv. 72–279. Height of handle, 0.15 m.

FIGURE 80:
Fragmentary scalloped bowl, outside of the handle. Inv. 72–279.

The first (Figs. 73–75) shows how the local potter worked.[161] He borrowed the essential shape of an Ionic cup, a form he knew from imported examples, and retained its high slanting rim and full-rounded body. A low conical foot, a type common at Poggio Civitate, was substituted for the Ionic ring foot; next he eliminated the horizontal tubular handles of the Ionic bowl and substituted a complicated double handle. Both faces of these double handles were mold-made—one in the form of a winged woman (Fig. 74) who grasps her long tresses at her chest and the other a stylized plaque outlined with spirals (Fig. 75). The two faces of the handles were surmounted by a rounded topknot which becomes a hat for the woman.

A second, similarly elaborate, local bucchero cup, also with a low conical foot and a complicated molded handle, has a fluted bowl substituted for the rounded Ionic body (Figs. 76–78).[162] The molded female figure on the handle, holding winglike objects—not long braids—at her chest, wears a tight-fitting skirt, bound at her waist by a rounded belt, and a long cloak which falls down her back and puffs out near her knees (Fig. 77). Particularly fine details, difficult to see in photographs, are the woman's multiple earrings; they are made with small clay dots placed up the side of each ear. The inside plaque of the handle is an elaborately molded tree-of-life pattern (Fig. 78). Just

as on the handle of the previous cup (Fig. 74), a rounded topknot, serving as a turban for the female figure, sits at the point where the two sections of the handle are joined. The earrings and tree-of-life suggest Near Eastern influences.

The third cup, preserved in a series of badly burned joining fragments, is the most complicated (Figs. 79 and 80).[163] The body of the bowl is decorated with deep, round scallops. We suspect that it originally had a low conical foot, preserved only by its attachment scar. The handle is formed with two molded women (similar to that of Fig. 74), joined at the level of their heads. Both are winged and clasp long braids at their chest. Instead of a turbanlike knob, the heads are surmounted by a third head, in the form of a woman with a high-crested helmet. This bowl is not unique because two other identical helmeted female heads have been found within the debris on Piano del Tesoro.

These cups or bowls with molded handles are very refined and all are from the same local workshops. Although certain stylistic traits are shared with the pottery from Southern Etruria, their style is independent: they are distant cousins of early pieces from Cerveteri and Veii.

The fourth unusual cup is also fluted and has a low conical foot.[164] Instead of a molded handle in the form of a female figure, however, it has a plain double strap handle pierced at the top of

FIGURE 83:
Small bucchero plate with horizontal rim and low ring
base. Side view. Inv. 73–6. Height, 0.02 m.

FIGURE 84:
Bucchero plate on high conical foot. Inv. 72–357.
Diam. 0.20 m.

FIGURE 81:
Small bucchero plate with horizontal rim and low
ring base. Top view. Inv. 70–100. Diam., 0.11 m.

FIGURE 82:
Small bucchero plate with horizontal rim and
low ring base. Bottom view. Inv. 70–100.

FIGURE 85:
Bucchero bowl on high conical foot. Inv. 73–36.
Height, 0.09 m.

FIGURE 86:
Lid for bucchero bowl. Inv. 73–291.
Height, 0.06 m.

FIGURE 88:
Buccheroid bowl on high conical foot. Inv. 71–321.
Height, 0.12 m.

FIGURE 87:
Covered bowl on a low foot. Inv. 73–240.
Height of bowl, 0.03 m.

FIGURE 89:
Buccheroid lid with impressed rosettes.
Inv. 71–613. Diam., 0.20 m.

its arch by a small hole. A voluted finial, with a hole rising into its central shaft, was found in the same debris layer as the badly burned bowl (Figs. 79 and 80). Nielsen realized that this voluted member was the fluted cup's finial and that it could be put on and taken off at will.

Local Bucchero/Buccheroid Pottery. A series of unusual bucchero and buccheroid wares, all local in fabric, decoration, and form, may have served specialized functions. The small plates, either on low ring bases or high conical feet, could have held small portions of exotic foods. Covered bowls of different shapes and sizes may have kept foods either hot or cold; or perhaps they held honey or sweet sauces from one day to the next. One unique small pitcher may even have held oil or vinegar for dressing salads or boiled foods such as grain. As expected, pitchers for wine, although not common, occur in local fabrics. Naturally, many of these functional forms also exist in imported fabrics. Most conspicuous are the Ionic and Laconian II bowls mentioned above;[165] however, pitchers, plates, and oil flasks also exist in Italo-Corinthian fabrics. Two small plates with low ring bases and wide horizontal rims are nearly intact. The rim of the first[166] is decorated with incised circles and rosettes (Figs. 81 and 82); that of the second is graced by three applied plastic ornaments (Fig. 83).[167] The horizontal rim of a third plate, elevated on a high conical foot, is decorated

with a fine net pattern.[168] This pattern was impressed, perhaps with a specialized incised conical tool. The same refined net pattern occurs on many fragmentary pots from the Orientalizing levels of Piano del Tesoro. These small plates on high conical feet are more common in the Orientalizing period than their larger relatives; however, those do occur. One bucchero piece, heavily burned and missing its conical base, has a central depression and a rim edged with a delicate impressed guilloche (Fig. 84).[169] This series may be the direct ancestor of a number of bucchero (or buccheroid) bowls and plates on high conical feet. One well-preserved example illustrates the more full-bodied type (Fig. 85).[170]

Covered bowls, though they are not always easy to identify, make up part of the local dining sets. The base of a small example could pass for a low bowl except that its rim has an inner groove into which sits precisely a high-domed cover with a sturdy lifting knob (Figs. 86 and 87).[171] A larger covered bowl (Figs. 88 and 89) has a lid, mistakenly published as a bowl;[172] it was carefully constructed so that the lid, decorated with small rosettes, fits over a vertical rim and comes to rest on a special ledge at the pot's shoulder. This local serving piece is one of our more interesting pots. Two other small bowls perhaps originally had lids. The first, found within a mixed context, is a black buccheroid, straight-sided bowl on a

FIGURE 95:
Etrusco-Corinthian globular aryballos. Inv. 71–779. Height, 0.07 m.

FIGURE 97:
Etrusco-Corinthian plate, side view. Inv. 68–552. Height, 0.05 m.

FIGURE 98:
Etrusco-Corinthian plate, bottom view. Inv. 68–552. Diam.,0.23 m.

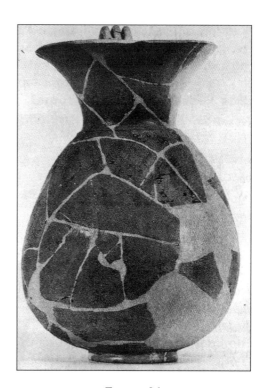

FIGURE 96:
Etrusco-Corinthian oinochoe, front view. Inv. 69–279. Height, 0.19 m.

FIGURE 99:
Etrusco-Corinthian plate, fr., by the American Academy Painter. Inv. 71–778. Pres. Dim., 0.09 x 0.05 m.

at Poggio Civitate were brought to the site filled with oil, not wine;[182] small aryballoi such as this frequently could have been filled from that supply. The masterpiece of Etrusco-Corinthian pottery from Poggio Civitate is an oinochoe with wide-flaring rim, full-rounded body, low ring base, and handle made from three delicate tubular sections; its shoulder zone is decorated with a boldly incised scale pattern (Fig. 96).[183] The shape and decoration recall the best of Protocorinthian, and I do not hesitate to date the piece as early as 650–625 B.C. A series of low plates flush out the Etrusco-Corinthian pots from Murlo. One complete example, found in the debris covering the western flank, is simply decorated (Figs. 97 and 98),[184] although others are painted with typical domestic fowl. One fragment, by the American Academy Painter, shows the type (Fig. 99).[185]

Utility Wares. The largest class of pottery from the site is comprised of utility wares, generally made from coarse impasto. These pieces are the ordinary pots used to prepare, serve, and store dry and liquid foods.[186] Thrown and hand-made pieces, varying in size from small cups (Fig. 100)[187] to large storage jars nearly a half-meter high,[188] abound and demonstrate the vitality of this most basic craft at Murlo. Many pieces, such as two carefully thrown and burnished storage jars, are beautiful examples of meticulously crafted kitchen wares.[189] Others are ill-shaped copies of more elegant and refined dining wares.[190] All attest to the importance attached to the storage and preparation of food, and indicate the extensive nature of dining at the site.[191] A very few specific examples give a brief glimpse of these sturdy and solid pieces.

A coarse impasto pitcher, with a distinctive tubular handle, is one of the more robust shapes (Fig. 101).[192] A few storage jars, made from coarse local clay frequently containing bits of gravel and mica, are typical of their class. The first, made from an orange-brown impasto, is rather thin and was fired irregularly (Fig. 102).[193] The second (Fig. 103) and third (Fig. 104) are heavier and thicker.[194] The fourth is even larger and heavier.[195] All four are Bouloumié's Form M. A final storage jar may once have had a lid (Fig. 105).[196]

It is difficult, if not impossible, to establish what these storage jars could have contained and exactly how they were used. Certainly nuts, grains, dried fruits, and berries are foods which could easily have been kept in them for a number of months. Oils and fats, honey, salted fish and meats, and foods concentrated by boiling also may have been put down for storage in jars. There are no local amphorae or, for that matter, any other shapes in which wine could have been kept, and I wonder if that beverage was used at the site. The large jars, and there are a number which measure over 0.50 m in height, could have been used for making beer or mead, both of which are well documented in Celtic and Germanic drinking rituals. They, rather than wine, may have been the normal fare at Murlo.

Bouloumié has identified a number of terracotta pieces which he associates with the kitchen. Included within the series are cooking bells of various sizes (Fig. 106),[197] portable braziers (Fig. 107),[198] and a curious group of large pots pierced by holes (Fig. 108).[199] The one complete example has been interpreted as a cooking stand or lantern, and by Charlotte Scheffer as a planting pot.[200] These pieces, rarely documented from Etruscan sites, give glimpses of the mundane daily activities such as cooking and preparing foods. Other clay utensils, many of which have been noted in previous reports, include net- and loom-weights,[201] clay bobbins (rocchetti),[202] scrapers,[203] and spindle whorls or impasto beads.[204] I include an illustration of one spindle whorl in order to document the linear decoration on its underside (Figs. 109 and 110).[205]

The making of pottery, pithoi, and architectural terracottas are related skills. Even though no kilns have been found, most clay objects were certainly made locally.[206] These products probably did not circulate far from Poggio Civitate even though an occasional cup, stamped rocchetto, or spindle whorl may have been taken home by a visitor to the site.

Local Products Other Than Clay Objects

Metal

Other crafts, more specialized and aimed at a wider market, thrived on Piano del Tesoro, probably during both occupation periods. Most of the small iron and bronze pieces were made locally.[207] A bronze duck (Fig. 111)[208] and an implement (Fig. 112)[209] are two of the finer pieces. Of special interest are the bronze nails, tacks, fish hooks, rings, etc., which were made for local consumption. The most elaborate iron and bronze objects from Murlo are fibulae and buckles, the latter displaying an unusual technique of iron inlaid into bronze.[210]

Jewelry

Two small serpentine gemstones, pierced for suspension, may have been carved at the site because the stone has been identified as local to the area of Murlo. The smaller is olive-drab and is decorated with shallow incisions (Inv. 75–99). On one face is a lion, walking right, dangling a

FIGURE 100:
Small impasto
hand-made cup.
Inv. 68–417.
Height, 0.06 m.

FIGURE 101:
Impasto pitcher
with tubular
handle. Inv.
67–126.
Height, 0.19 m.

FIGURE 102:
Small impasto
jar. Inv.
79–261.
Height, 0.09 m.

FIGURE 103:
Medium-sized
impasto storage
jar. Inv.
76–173.

FIGURE 104:
Medium-sized
impasto storage
jar. Inv.
79–266.
Height, 0.25 m.

FIGURE 105
Two-handled
storage jar. Inv.
79–268.
Height, 0.21 m.

FIGURE 106:
Large terracotta cooking bell.
Inv. 76–174. Height, 0.12 m.

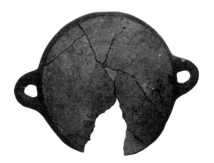

FIGURE 107:
Large terracotta brazier. Inv. 71–151.
Diam, 0.33 m.

FIGURE 108:
Terracotta cooking stand or lantern (?), or planting pot (?).
Inv. 73–137. Height, 0.36 m.

FIGURE 109:
Spindle
whorl, side
view. Inv.
76–55. Height,
0.02 m.

FIGURE 110:
Spindle whorl,
bottom view.
Inv. 76–55.
Diam., 0.02 m.

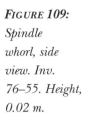

human leg from his mouth, and on the other is a dancing, ithyphallic male; both figures are crudely incised.[211] The second gem is a soft, jadelike blue-green color; two lions attack a wild boar, one lion on each side (Fig. 113).[212] This badly worn gem was mutilated by a hole drilled through the boar from front to back, perhaps so that the piece could be suspended. The base of the gem is engraved with a delicate pattern of dolphins, a griffin, and a hippocamp.

Other precious jewelry found within the Orientalizing destruction levels sealed under the floors of the Archaic Meeting Hall include two very small silver fibulae (Inv. 71–618 and 71–669),[213] fragments of a delicate gold bracelet (Fig. 114)[214] and other small gold ornaments. Although we cannot establish where these gold and silver pieces were made, they are probably products of Northern Etruria. Their delicate forms recall some of the finer pieces from Vetulonia and Quinto Fiorentino, and especially a series of gold rosettes on a gold band from the latter site.[215]

Bone and Ivory Objects

The largest group of luxury items found in the destruction layers of the Orientalizing Long Building are a series of small bone and ivory ornamental plaques and three-dimensional figures. These have been extensively published, and only a few will be illustrated here, even though all are of high quality and interest. The first found was a small sleeping animal (Fig. 115) probably made from ivory, which turned whitish gray when heated to a high temperature by the fire which consumed the building.[216] The charm of the piece lies in the artist's ability to capture the essence of a small, completely tranquil, sleeping animal.

Other masterpieces of this early school of ivory carving, which Nielsen locates at Murlo, are crouching or reclining animals. A ram (Fig. 116)[217] and two sphinxes fully display the delicacy and quality of the workmanship. One sphinx was heated to the point where it turned entirely black,[218] and the other (Fig. 117) was toasted brown to black.[219] Nielsen considers another ivory from the site to be by the same hand as the two sphinxes. The piece is a fragmentary plaque, in the form of a lion, which preserves only the head; on the back is a boldly incised Etruscan inscription with the name Avil (Figs. 118 and 119).[220] A bone plaque, a Gorgoneion with its tongue lolling between large fanglike teeth, may have been a furniture inlay (Fig. 120).[221] A bone lady, completely wrapped in a long mantle, may be a small, household devotional figurine (Fig. 121).[222] The last animal from Poggio Civitate illustrated here is a magnificent, perfectly preserved miniature griffin figurine (Fig. 122).[223] The boldness of design and execution place this miniature piece among the very

FIGURE 115:
Ivory sleeping animal.
Inv. 71–282. Height, 0.02 m.

FIGURE 116:
Crouching ivory ram. Inv. 71–92.
Length, 0.03 m.

FIGURE 117:
Crouching ivory sphinx. Inv.
71–198. Height, 0.02 m.

FIGURE 118:
Ivory lion plaque, fr. of head.
Inv. 71–500. Height, 0.01 m.

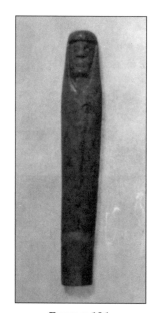

FIGURE 121:
Bone woman, perhaps a
devotional figure. Inv. 71–100.
Height, 0.06 m.

FIGURE 119:
Ivory lion plaque, fr. of head, back
side with Etruscan inscription, mi
avil. Inv. 71–500.

FIGURE 120:
Bone plaque in the form of a
Gorgoneion. Inv. 71–102.
Height, 0.02 m.

FIGURE 122:
Ivory or bone griffin. Inv.
71–101. Height, 0.02 m.

Part III

CONCLUSIONS: AN INTERPRETATION OF POGGIO CIVITATE

I have attempted to document the remains found on Poggio Civitate and to suggest, through illustrations of the objects, how the site must have appeared during its existence. We now must face the dilemma which all archaeologists encounter. Is it possible to interpret a complex series of physical objects—architecture, pottery, etc.— except in the most basic terms? We can usually identify the pottery from a site, establish its place of manufacture, place it within a chronological framework, and, if we have enough examples, we may even postulate how it was used. The same may be done with other objects such as bronze, ivory, and precious metals. Can we take those same objects, however, place them within an historical context, and interpret their significance? Frequently an archaeologist or historian may turn to related monuments that might help clarify his or her site. Unfortunately, very few

parallels exist for the buildings on Piano del Tesoro. Our interpretation of the site must be made directly from what has been found. Perhaps by asking the proper questions we can reconstruct the life of the site and understand its historical, cultural, and artistic importance. All who venture on this intellectual path, the attempt to understand a complex site primarily from its physical remains, must recognize that they are treating physical objects as if they were texts; they are making the assumption that objects may be "read," and they are attempting to create written history from non-verbal sources. Those who undertake such exercises cannot cancel out their own cultural background, and many of their own cultural values will automatically influence their thinking.

In this general review I have attempted to explain and document the broad aspects of the excavations at Poggio

Civitate and to illustrate the site's physical remains, including its architecture and small finds. I have expressed my opinion that Murlo was the center of a Northern League which existed from about 675 to 550/530 B.C., and that both the Orientalizing and Archaic complex were primarily the seat and meeting halls for this league. (These broad dates are suggested by the earliest bucchero[225] and the latest Greek pottery.[226]) I argued in 1970 that the ritual destruction of the site proved its political importance and established that it was a respected and feared center of Northern Etruria.[227] At that time, and I continue to hold this view, I suggested that Poggio Civitate was deliberately destroyed during the second half of the sixth century B.C. by the rulers of Chiusi so that they could consolidate their power and eliminate a rival center. This ritual destruction, in which the Archaic buildings were torn down and their terracotta revetments buried under layers of earth and small stones, was an attempt to put Poggio Civitate out of bounds forever and to place a tabu on the area occupied by the Meeting Hall on Piano del Tesoro. This *damnatio* was highly successful; no lasting occupation took place on Poggio Civitate from the late sixth century B.C. to the present. The importance of the site, perhaps as a religious or political center, was on the other hand never completely forgotten because the names *Poggio Civitate* and *Civita Magna* remain associated with this hill until this day. The name Poggio Civitate, documented during the early Medieval period, indicates that the local inhabitants were aware of the importance of the site and perhaps knew that it should not be disturbed.

This view of Poggio Civitate has developed over twenty years of gradual study of its materials. I have come to believe that there is one continuous occupation at the site, and that there was no cultural break between the destruction of the Orientalizing buildings and the construction and occupation of the Archaic ones. Furthermore, I think that the destruction of the Orientalizing buildings was a casual event. Therefore, I assume that the Archaic buildings followed directly on the Orientalizing and served the same functions. If we understand the Archaic complex as a well-organized set of buildings which was the seat of a Northern Etruscan League and served as a place for its meetings, the Orientalizing buildings presumably would have had the same function.

The Archaic Meeting Hall, with its regular plan and complicated iconographical program of terracotta decoration, accents the importance of the site. The Archaic complex may have been planned by a master architect who directed its layout and construction. I wonder how long it took to build it and how many men were required to carry out its completion. The resources of one family, even if it owned a large estate, would have been strained by such a costly undertaking. If the site was the seat of a league, however, the league's members could have supplied the manpower and funds to replace its destroyed meeting halls. If one assumes that the members of the league were within two-days' walking distance from Poggio Civitate, a number of sites which have produced late Orientalizing material fall under the theoretical sphere of Murlo. These centers include ancient centers located near the modern localities of Castelnuovo Tancredi, Pompana, Pari, Camigliano, Montalcino, Buonconvento, Asciano, Castelnuovo Berardegna, Rosia, Siena, and perhaps even Monteriggioni, Castellina in Chianti, Colle Val d'Elsa, Casole d'Elsa, Pienza, and San Casciano Val di Pesa.

Now that we have established that local craftsmen thrived on Poggio Civitate during the Orientalizing period, the same activity should be expected during the Archaic period. I think the number of fine ivory, bone, bronze, and refined pieces of local pottery indicate a trade in souvenirs similar to that found in any present-day religious or tourist site. Trinkets would have been as avidly purchased in antiquity as they are now. And, just as now, they would have been taken home and treasured. This local industry could have been a major source of income for the inhabitants at the site, many of whom must have been free artisans and skilled craftsmen. I see no evidence for slaves.

One of the most difficult theoretical problems of the site is the social status of its inhabitants. It is easy to assume, following Marxist thinking, that the objects found in the destruction of the Orientalizing buildings were owned by a particular individual or family; and then to assume that the family was a wealthy, aristocratic one which, because of its love for imported objects, was in contact with Southern Etruria and even the Greek world. But how do we know this? The building could have been the residence of a caretaker of the League, not its owner, and the trappings could have been used by that individual or others attending specific functions at the center. We know that certain Greek states provided meals and dining equipment for magistrates. Perhaps a similar practice occurred at Poggio Civitate. Religious festivals centering on a particular shrine are still common in Italy. Norman Douglas describes such a gathering at Castrovillari capturing the spirit of such festivals, and I suspect that a meeting of the League at Poggio Civitate had many points in common with this modern *festa*.[228]

Certain scholars of a Marxist bent have assumed that the Archaic Building Complex was the residence of a local ruler, a minor dynast who lived in regal splendor. If this were the case, I would expect to have found extensive evidence of a palace society—large storage rooms, tools, arms, and even special areas for ceremonial functions. None of these are present even though there is sufficient evidence that masses of people frequented the site, gathered in its spacious buildings, used and discarded large amounts of common dining wares, and purchased local crafts.

I am well aware that I am interpreting the same archaeological materials, buildings, and small objects in a very different way from certain of my European colleagues. It may be instructive to look beyond the archaeological materials to our diverse cultural heritage.

An Italian, especially a Tuscan, could logically understand the large, complex, and highly organized Archaic buildings of Poggio Civitate as the residence of a local noble whose estate would have had servants to work the soil and craftsmen to produce objects for commercial transactions and trade. Underlying this concept of a noble and servants is the permanent and real value of the land, which has been under cultivation for centuries. Even though there is no evidence that Poggio Civitate was the residence of a large landowner, that conclusion is drawn automatically when one thinks of the country estates, such as Pentolina, Frosini, or Casone, within the area of rural Siena.

I see the same material in a different light. My ancestors settled parts of West Virginia at a time when land was plentiful and could easily be accumulated. These American pioneer families could, and frequently did, lay claim to holdings equal to those of a major Tuscan estate. Only a small portion of their land was worked by the owner and his family, however, and the remainder was frequently held in reserve for division among children. Families lived independently and often at considerable distances one from the other, and only came together on Sundays at churches which served as the centers of local society. No one in that society was either noble or aristocratic; they were farmers, and the land which they claimed was plentiful even though forested. The next higher center, after the local church or meeting house, was the county seat, a town which may have been quite small and whose primary function was to house the county court. If we fuse these two meeting spots of early America, the local church and the court, we may have an institution similar to that which has been found on Poggio Civitate. Although we know little about the Etruscan society of the seventh and early sixth century B.C. in Northern Etruria, I suspect that the land was covered with thick forests and that the society resembled that of any culture living in balance with its natural surroundings. I doubt that the inhabitants of the areas around

Poggio Civitate dominated the land as did the estate owners of Renaissance Tuscany.

I recognize that my interpretation of Poggio Civitate as the seat of a Northern League cannot be proven; however, it meets all the conditions of the site, and I think that I can understand what we have found more easily by falling back on that explanation than on one requiring an aristocratic society with ruler, servants, and slaves.

Notes

Introduction

1. *Monumenti Antichi*, Vol. 30 (1925).

2. *Notizie degli Scavi di Antichità*, 1926, 165–170.

3. *Carta Archeologica al 100.000, Foglio 120 (Siena), II, N.E.* (Florence 1927).

4. Riesch in *Studi Etruschi* 8 (1934), 335–337; *Poggio Civitate* 1970a-b, nos. 3s–9s, pls. II–V.

5. See also Edlund 1987, 88, Ill. 12.

Part I

6. Phillips 1966, 1967a and 1967b.

7. Phillips 1966, 7, fig. 2. [For a discussion of the local names Piano del Tesoro and Civita Magna, see Rowland, in press.]

8. For a companion piece see Phillips 1967a, pl. 44, fig. 24.

9. Phillips 1966, 8, fig. 4.

10. Phillips 1966, 12, fig. 12.

11. Phillips 1967a, pl. 40, fig. 3.

12. Phillips 1966, 8, fig. 5.

13. Phillips 1967a, pl. 40, figs. 3 and 5.

14. Phillips 1967a, pl. 40, figs. 7 and 10.

15. Phillips 1966, 8, fig. 4.

16. Phillips 1972, 250, Ill. 5 and Siena *CP*, 1985, 68, fig. 5.

17. Siena *CP*, 1985, 64–68. See also Edlund 1987, 89, fig. 8 A–B.

18. Phillips 1971a, 257.

19. Nielsen 1987, 91 n.2, observes that the same Oscan/Italic foot was used in the Stoa Workshops to the south of the Archaic Building Complex.

20. Siena CP, 1985, 64–69. [See also, Edlund-Berry 1991. The site of Satricum is particularly important for the question of monumental buildings, see Maaskant-Kleibrink 1987 and Maaskant-Kleibrink 1991, 103.]

21. Edlund 1987, esp. 87–92.

22. Phillips 1972, 251.

23. Nielsen and Phillips 1983 [1986] and Siena CP, 1985, 65–68, figs. 2–5.

24. Siena CP, 1985, 66–67; Nielsen and Phillips 1983 [1986], 11.

25. Nielsen and Phillips 1983 [1986], 17–24.

26. Nielsen 1987, figs. 1–11.

27. Nielsen 1987, 118–119. [See also, *Nielsen 1989 and Rick Gore, "The Eternal Etruscans," *National Geographic* 173:6 (June 1988), 697–743, ill. of unfired tiles with footprints on p. 718.]

28. Nielsen and Phillips 1983 [1986], 11.

29. Phillips 1985, 7. [Cf. Scheffer 1990.]

30. Phillips 1967A, pl. 40, figs. 5 and 8.

31. Rystedt 1983, 90, fig. 52.

32. Phillips 1967A, 40, fig. 9.

33. Phillips 1969A, 337, Ill. 2.

34. Phillips 1969A, 337, Ill. 2.

35. Phillips 1967A, pl. 39, fig. 4.

36. Phillips 1970A, pl. 54, fig. 9.

37. Phillips 1967A, pl. 40, figs. 3 and 8; Phillips 1968A, pl. 45, fig. 1.

38. Phillips 1968A, pl. 45, fig. 1.

39. Phillips 1980; Siena CP, 1985, 98–99.

40. Tobey, Nielsen, and Rowe 1984 [1986].

41. Wikander in Siena CP, 1985, 99, nos. 216–224: Wikander's no. 216 (Inv. 72–147) is a good example of the type, Nielsen and Phillips 1976, 126, fig. 13.

42. Inv. 67–411 and 68–200: Edlund (Gantz) 1972, 220 ff, no. 1. and Siena CP, 1985, 103–105 and nos. 258 and 263. [For the complete publication of these statues, see **Edlund-Berry 1992.]

43. Inv. 66–297: Edlund (Gantz) 1972, 229, no. 8, figs. 16–20.

44. Inv. 80–104: Edlund in Siena CP, 1985, 106, no. 271.

45. Inv. 66–297: Edlund (Gantz) 1972, 229, no. 8, figs. 18–20.

46. Inv. 69–200: Edlund (Gantz) 1972, 227, no. 6, figs. 12–14 and Edlund in Siena CP, 1985, 107, no. 276.

47. Inv. 67–425: Edlund in Siena CP, 1985, 109, no. 292.

48. SIENA *CP*, 1985, 102.
[The interpretation of
the total number of
fragments suggests that
we have evidence of at
least twenty statues with
an equal division
between male and
female figures; see
**EDLUND-BERRY 1992
and EDLUND-BERRY,
"The Murlo Cowboy," IN
PRESS.]

49. Inv. 71–307: EDLUND
(GANTZ) 1972, 234–235,
no. 11, figs. 29–34 and
water color opposite fig.
34 and Edlund in SIENA
CP, 1985, 105, no. 264.

50. Inv. 69–278: *POGGIO
CIVITATE* 1970A–B, no.
11, pl. 15a and SIENA
CP, 1985, 107, no. 274.

51. Inv. 71–330: SIENA *CP*,
1985, 107, no. 275.

52. Inv. 69–229: *POGGIO
CIVITATE* 1970A–B, no.
10, pl. 15b and SIENA
CP, 1985, 107, no. 272.

53. Inv. 70–177: PHILLIPS
1971A, 260, pl. 57, figs.
18–19.

54. Inv. 68–500: FULLERTON
1982, and SIENA *CP*,
1985, 110–111, no. 304,
and color detail on
cover.

55. Inv. 68–635: SIENA *CP*,
1985, 112, no. 305.

56. Inv. 68–100: *POGGIO
CIVITATE* 1970A–B, 30,
no. 9; SIENA *CP*, 1985,
108–109, no. 280; and
EDLUND 1985A.

57. Phillips in *POGGIO
CIVITATE* 1970A–B, 29.

58. BIANCHI BANDINELLI AND
GIULIANO 1973A, 196,
accepted this reasoning
and also dated the
statue late in the sixth
century.

59. GANTZ 1971, pl. V.

60. See also SIENA *CP*, 1985,
111–112, nos. 304–305.

61. L. Ronald Lacy in SIENA
CP, 1985, 110–114, nos.
306–326.

62. Inv. 68–280: *POGGIO
CIVITATE* 1970A–B, no.
23, pl. 20b; SIENA *CP*,
1985, 113–114, no. 325.

63. Inv. 78–79: NIELSEN AND
PHILLIPS 1983 [1986],
20–21, figs. 13–14; SIENA
CP, 1985, 113, no. 322.

64. Inv. 66–259: *POGGIO
CIVITATE* 1970A–B, 33,
no. 22, pl. 20a and
SIENA *CP*, 1985,
112–113, no. 315.

65. Inv. 70–313: NIELSEN
AND PHILLIPS 1983
[1986], 22–23, fig. 15.

66. Inv. 68–172: SIENA *CP*,
1985, 112, no. 308.

67. Inv. 68–510: NIELSEN
AND PHILLIPS 1976, 124
and 126, fig. 8; SIENA
CP, 1985, 112, no. 310.

68. Inv. 67–79: PHILLIPS
1969B, 50, fig. 18; SIENA
CP, 1985, 113, no. 316.

69. SMALL 1971, 46.

70. MERITT 1970.

71. NEILS 1976.

72. Inv. 68–68: *POGGIO
CIVITATE* 1970A–B, 44,
no. 81; NEILS 1976, p.
12, no. 11; and Lacy in
SIENA *CP*, 1985, 114, no.
327.

73. Inv. 72–235: Neils 1976, 8, no. 1 (the hair fragments and the tile backer were added to the piece after Neils' publication); Siena *CP*, 1985, 114–115, no. 328 (the photo of this piece on 115 is mistakenly labeled no. 327).

74. Inv. 67–10: *Poggio Civitate* 1970 a–b, 47, no. 92; Neils 1976, 20, no. 29, pl. 10,1; and Lacy in Siena *CP*, 1985, 115–116, no. 336.

75. Inv. 68–220: *Poggio Civitate* 1970a–b, 47, no. 93, pl. 33; Neils 1976, 20, no. 30, pl. 10,3; and Siena *CP*, 1985, 115–116, no. 337.

76. Inv. 68–150: *Poggio Civitate* 1970a–b, 42, no. 72, pl. 30; Meritt 1970, pl. 2b; Siena *CP*, 1985, 116–117, no. 338. [See Massa-Pairault, manuscript. For Archaic Etruscan simas, see Wikander, in press.]

77. Siena *CP*, 1985, 117–118, nos. 339, 338, and 341.

78. Inv. 68–148: Nielsen and Phillips 1976, 138, fig. 26; Siena *CP*, 1985, 117–118, no. 340.

79. Meritt 1970; Phillips in Siena *CP*, 1985, 118–121. [See also, **Phillips 1990. For an interpretation of the Lateral Sima at Poggio Civitate, see Nielsen, in press.]

80. Inv. 67–20 and 68–120: *Poggio Civitate* 1970a–b, 39, nos. 44 and 52 and Siena *CP*, 1985, 118, no. 345.

81. Inv. 68–178: Unpublished. [See **Damgaard Andersen 1990, 70, figs. 17–18.]

82. [See **Damgaard Andersen 1990.]

83. [See **Phillips 1990.]

84. Inv. 68–120: [See **Phillips 1990, 141, figs. 1a–c, and 155, no. 1; Damgaard Andersen 1990, 67, no. 5, figs. 10–11.]

85. Inv. 68–504: Winter 1978, 34, pl. 10, 1.2. [**Phillips 1990, 148, fig. 21, 156, no. 8.]

86. Inv. 68–152: Winter 1977, 28, n. 27; Inv. 68–504: Winter 1977, 26–27, pl. 8.3 and 9.3; Winter 1978, 34 and pl. 10, 1.2, and Phillips in Siena *CP*, 1985, 119, no. 356. [For Inv. 68–152, see **Phillips 1990, 153, figs. 36–37, 157, no. 24.]

87. Inv. 66–247: *Poggio Civitate* 1970a–b, 39, no. 47; Nielsen and Phillips 1974, 267, Ill. 1; Siena *CP*, 1985, 121, no. 374. [See also, Phillips 1990, 143–144, figs. 6–7, 155, no. 3.]

88. Inv. 71–170: Siena *CP*, 1985, 121, no. 375.

89. Nielsen and Phillips 1974, 267.

90. Nielsen 1987, 117, fig. 86.

91. Inv. 68–195: *Poggio Civitate* 1970a–b, 40, no. 59; Winter 1977, 31–32, pl. 12, figs. 2–3; Phillips in Siena *CP*, 1985, 121, no. 376.

92. Phillips 1969a, 335.

93. Inv. 70–129: WINTER 1977, 28, pl. 11, figs. 2–4; Phillips in SIENA *CP*, 1985, 119, no. 358. [See **PHILLIPS 1990, 153–154, fig. 40, 157, no. 25.]

94. MERITT 1970.

95. SIENA *CP*, 1985, 122–123, nos. 385–436. [See also, RATHJE, IN PRESS.]

96. Inv. 69–220: *POGGIO CIVITATE* 1970A–B, 56, no. 114; SIENA *CP*, 1985, 125, no. 407.

97. SMALL 1971.

98. MACINTOSH 1974, 27, fig. 2.

99. MERITT 1970, 21–23, figs. 6–8.

100. ROOT 1973, 137.

101. GANTZ 1974.

102. Inv. 69–384: NIELSEN AND PHILLIPS 1976, 145, fig. 35; Rathje in SIENA *CP*, 1985, 125–126, no. 425.

103. Inv. 66–231: *POGGIO CIVITATE* 1970A–B, 59, no. 123, pl. 39a; Rathje in SIENA *CP*, 1985, 126, no. 429.

104. MACINTOSH 1974, fig. 3.

105. FABRICOTTI 1977–1979 [1980].

106. G. Giglioli, *L'Arte etrusca* (1935) pl. 236, fig. 1 and 237, fig. 4.

107. GANTZ 1971.

108. Inv. 68–264; *POGGIO CIVITATE* 1970A–B, 57–58, no. 115, Rathje in SIENA *CP*, 1985, 125, no. 417; MACINTOSH 1974, fig. 1.

109. GANTZ 1971.

110. THUILLIER 1980.

111. CRISTOFANI 1975.

112. TORELLI 1980 [1983].

113. PHILLIPS 1983 and in SIENA *CP*, 1985, 121–122, nos. 379–384.

114. Inv. 70–200: PHILLIPS 1983, 2, no. 2, figs. 5–9 and SIENA *CP*, 1985, 122, no. 380.

115. Inv. 68–161: SIENA *CP*, 1985, 122, no. 381.

116. Inv. 71–167: SIENA *CP*, 1985, 151, no. 688. [See also, **EDLUND-BERRY 1989B, 24, no. 3, figs. 9–12.]

117. Inv. 67–450: SIENA *CP*, 1985, 151–152, no. 689; WARDEN 1977.

118. Phillips in *POGGIO CIVITATE* 1970A–B, 79–80.

119. Phillips in SIENA *CP*, 1985, 78, nos. 52–53. [See also, PHILLIPS 1989A, 32, figs. 27–30.]

120. Phillips in *POGGIO CIVITATE* 1970A–B, 79–80. [See also, EDLUND-BERRY, IN PRESS.]

PART II

121. Inv. 71–106: PHILLIPS 1973B; THUILLIER 1985, 70–77; WARDEN 1985, 89, pl. 19; Warden in SIENA *CP*, 1985, 90, no. 146.

122. Inv. 71–105: PHILLIPS 1973B; THUILLIER 1985, 70–77; WARDEN 1985, 89, pl. 18; Warden in SIENA *CP*, 1985, 90, no. 145.

123. Inv. 71–393: PHILLIPS 1980, 204 and Phillips in SIENA *CP*, 1985, 75, no. 30. [See also, PHILLIPS 1989A, 30, fig. 2.]

124. Phillips in SIENA *CP*, 1985, 75–77, nos. 31–43. [See also, PHILLIPS 1989A.]

125. NIELSEN 1987.

126. NIELSEN AND PHILLIPS 1974, 268–270.

127. The relationship between the an of the Long Orientalizing Building and the Archaic Meeting Hall is discussed and illustrated by NIELSEN AND PHILLIPS 1974, 268 and Ill. 2 and in SIENA *CP*, 1985, 65, fig. 2.

128. SIENA *CP*, 1985, 64–65, figs. 1–2.

129. For a trench, showing the relationship of the Archaic and Orientalizing buildings, see NIELSEN 1987, 95, fig. 11.

130. SIENA *CP*, 1985, 47, fig. 8. [For Acquarossa, see VITERBO 1986 and the publications by Lundgren and Wendt, Rystedt, Scheffer, Strandberg Olofsson, Ch. Wikander and Ö. Wikander.]

131. NIELSEN 1987.

132. SIENA *CP*, 1985, 65, fig. 2, and NIELSEN AND PHILLIPS 1983 [1986], 11, fig. 4.

133. SIENA *CP*, 1985, 69–70, nos. 1–6. [See also, WIKANDER 1988 and WIKANDER, IN PREPARA-TION.]

134. Inv. 70–344: NIELSEN AND PHILLIPS 1974, 276, Ill. 14; RYSTEDT 1983, 39–41, fig. 18, pl. 14; Rystedt in SIENA *CP*, 1985, 70, no. 7 (for a review of RYSTEDT 1983, see RIDGWAY AND RIDGWAY 1984). [See also, RYSTEDT, IN PRESS.]

135. Inv. 71–310: RYSTEDT 1983, 41, fig. 19, pl. 15; Rystedt in SIENA *CP*, 1985, 70, no. 8.

136. Inv. 70–104: NIELSEN AND PHILLIPS 1974, 276, Ill. 14; RYSTEDT 1983, 43, fig. 23, pl. 18; Rystedt in SIENA *CP*, 1985, 71, no. 10.

137. Inv. 85–26 and 85–17: NIELSEN 1987, 95, figs. 12–13.

138. Inv. 69–284: RYSTEDT 1983, 35–36, fig. 15, pls. 9–10; Rystedt in SIENA *CP*, 1985, 71–72, no. 13; PHILLIPS 1985, 11, fig. 7.

139. Inv. 68–474 and 68–475: RYSTEDT 1983, 36 and 38, fig. 16, and pl. 11; and Rystedt in SIENA *CP*, 1985, 72, nos. 14–15.

140. RYSTEDT 1983, 36–38, fig. 16, and pl. 11; and Rystedt in SIENA *CP*, 1985, 72, nos. 14–15.

141. Inv. 70–110: Wikander in SIENA *CP*, 1985, 73, no. 21.

142. This system is known on a house model from Velletri now in the Villa Giulia: R.A. Staccioli, *Modelli di edifici etrusco-italici. I modelli votivi* (Florence 1968), no. 32.

143. Siena *CP*, 1985, 47–48 Acquarossa no. 23.

144. Orientalizing lateral simas occur at the site and have been partially published by Nielsen 1987. [See also, Nielsen 1985 [1989] and Nielsen, in press.]

145. [Nielsen 1985 [1989].]

146. Inv. 66–229: *Poggio Civitate* 1970a–b, 50, no. 101; Siena *CP*, 1985, 73, no. 24; Nielsen 1987, 106, figs. 50–53.

147. Inv. 68–196: *Poggio Civitate* 1970a–b, 46, no. 89; Phillips 1984; Siena *CP*, 1985, 73, no. 25; Nielsen 1987, 114–116, fig. 83.

148. Inv. 85–33: Nielsen 1987, 115–116, fig. 84.

149. For Ellen Simmon's reconstruction drawings of the Orientalizing lateral sima see Nielsen 1987, 114–115, figs. 81–82.

150. Inv. 68–50: *Poggio Civitate* 1970a–b, 33, no. 20 and Phillips in Siena *CP*, 1985, 150, no. 685. [See Winter, in press.]

151. Siena *CP*, 1985, 150.

152. Siena *CP*, 1985, 33 and 44, Acquarossa no. 9.

153. Siena *CP*, 1985, 53–54.

154. Siena *CP*, 1985, 43–50.

155. Classed by Bouloumié as Form E3B in Siena *CP*, 1985, 138.

156. Siena *CP*, 1985, 141, nos. 567–574.

157. Inv. 71–80: Bouloumié, Form C2 in Siena *CP*, 1985, 138, no. 547.

158. Inv. 71–71: Nielsen and Phillips 1976, 146, figs. 37a and 38; Siena *CP*, 1985, 80, no. 61.

159. Inv. 73–212: Nielsen and Phillips 1975, 364, Ill. 11, pl. 66, figs. 24–26; Siena *CP*, 1985, 80, no. 62.

160. Phillips in Siena *CP*, 1985, 74–77, nos. 30–45. [See also, Phillips 1989a.]

161. Inv. 72–280: Nielsen and Phillips 1975, 362–363, pl. 65, figs. 15–17; Siena *CP*, 1985, 81, no. 74.

162. Inv. 73–239: Nielsen and Phillips 1977a, 91–92, figs. 14–17; Siena *CP*, 1985, 83, no. 89.

163. Inv. 72–279: Nielsen and Phillips 1983 [1986], 16–17, figs. 8–9; Siena *CP*, 1985, 83, no. 95.

164. Inv. 73–314: Siena *CP*, 1985, 83, no. 86.

165. Phillips in Siena *CP*, 1985, 75–77, nos. 31–43. [See also, Phillips 1989a.]

166. Inv. 70–100: Phillips 1971a, 260, pl. 61; Siena *CP*, 1985, 85, no. 113.

167. Inv. 73–6: NIELSEN AND PHILLIPS 1974, 272, Ill. 8, pl. 57, figs. 12–14; SIENA *CP*, 1985, 85, no. 110.

168. Inv. 73–224: NIELSEN AND PHILLIPS 1977A, 90, Ill. 8, fig. 10; SIENA *CP*, 1985, 85, no. 116.

169. Inv. 72–357: SIENA *CP*, 1985, 85, no. 118.

170. Inv. 73–36: NIELSEN AND PHILLIPS 1975, 363, pl. 64, figs. 20–21; SIENA *CP*, 1985, 141, no. 582; Bouloumié Form F.

171. Inv. 73–240 and 73–291: SIENA *CP*, 1985, 86, no. 122.

172. Inv. 71–321 and 71–613: NIELSEN AND PHILLIPS 1975, 358–359, pl. 62, fig. 1. Lid on bowl in SIENA *CP*, 1985, 86, no. 120.

173. Inv. 68–11: *POGGIO CIVITATE* 1970A–B, 71, no. 183; SIENA *CP*, 1985, 141, no. 586.

174. Inv. 72–281: NIELSEN AND PHILLIPS 1974, 272, Ill. 9, pl. 58, fig. 15; SIENA *CP*, 1985, 86, no. 121.

175. Inv. 71–171: NIELSEN AND PHILLIPS 1983 [1986], 6 and 9, fig. 3a; SIENA *CP*, 1985, 88, no. 131. Note that the rosettes in the top row are smaller than those which circle the base.

176. Inv. 71–232: SIENA *CP*, 1985, 87, no. 127.

177. Inv. 71–825: NIELSEN AND PHILLIPS 1975, 359–360, Ills. 4–6, pl. 62, figs. 5–6; SIENA *CP*, 1985, 87, no. 129.

178. They may be reviewed in PHILLIPS 1980; Phillips in SIENA *CP*, 1985, 74–78, nos. 30–53. [See also, PHILLIPS 1989A.]

179. PHILLIPS 1980.

180. Elisabetta Mangani (SIENA *CP*, 1985, 78–80, nos. 54–59) accepts the Murlo chronology for the pieces.

181. Inv. 71–779: Mangani in SIENA *CP*, 1985, 79, no. 57.

182. Inv. 72–430 and 73–202: Phillips in SIENA *CP*, 1985, 75 and 77, nos. 46 and 47. [See also, PHILLIPS 1989A, 31, figs. 4–6 and 32, figs. 14–18.]

183. Inv. 69–279: *POGGIO CIVITATE* 1970A–B, 66, no. 152; Mangani in SIENA *CP*, 1985, 79–80, no. 58.

184. Inv. 68–552: Mangani in SIENA *CP*, 1985, 80, no. 59.

185. Inv. 71–778: NIELSEN AND PHILLIPS 1974, 271, pl. 56, fig. 8; Mangani in SIENA *CP*, 1985, 78, no. 55. For a recent discussion of the American Academy Painter, see a note by Szilágyi (PHILLIPS 1986, 154, n. 24).

186. Partially studied by Antoinette Bouloumié-Marique and Bernard Bouloumié (BOULOUMIÉ-MARIQUE 1978; Bouloumié in SIENA *CP*, 1985, 138–146, nos. 533–643).

187. Inv. 68–417: *POGGIO CIVITATE* 1970A–B, 72, no. 186; BOULOUMIÉ-MARIQUE 1978, 80, no. 527, pl. 12; SIENA *CP,* 1985, 141–142, no. 588.

188. SIENA *CP,* 1985, 144, no. 613.

189. Inv. 71–79: BOULOUMIÉ-MARIQUE 1978, 110, pl. 27; SIENA *CP,* 1985, 143, no. 600; Inv. 71–313: SIENA *CP,* 1985, 143, no. 602.

190. Inv. 68–551: SIENA *CP,* 1985, 140, no. 561.

191. The studies of Antoinette and Bernard Bouloumié must be consulted in order to understand the scope and importance of this local production.

192. Inv. 67–126: *POGGIO CIVITATE* 1970A–B, 72, no. 187; BOULOUMIÉ-MARIQUE 1978, 106, no. 535, pl. 24; SIENA *CP,* 1985, 146, no. 638.

193. Inv. 79–261: SIENA *CP,* 1985, 145, no. 628.

194. Inv. 76–173: unpublished. Inv. 79–266: SIENA *CP,* 1985, 144, no. 617.

195. Inv. 66–143: *POGGIO CIVITATE* 1970A–B, 73, no. 195; BOULOUMIÉ-MARIQUE 1978, 92, no. 537, pl. 18; SIENA *CP,* 1985, 144, no. 616.

196. Inv. 79–268: SIENA *CP,* 1985, 144, no. 612.

197. Inv. 76–174: SIENA *CP,* 1985, 147, no. 655.

198. Inv. 71–151: BOULOUMIÉ 1978, 122, no. 1160, fig. 2, pl. 2; SIENA *CP,* 1985, 147, no. 648.

199. Inv. 73–137: BOULOUMIÉ 1978, 114, no. 1150, fig. 1, and pl. 1; SIENA *CP,* 1985, 153, no. 694.

200. SIENA *CP,* 1985, 153, no. 694. [See also, SCHEFFER 1985.]

201. SIENA *CP,* 1985, 149, nos. 670–672.

202. SIENA *CP,* 1985, 149, nos. 682–683.

203. SIENA *ÇP,* 1985, 153–154, nos. 695–696.

204. SIENA *CP,* 1985, 149, nos. 673–681.

205. Inv. 76–55: SIENA *CP,* 1985, 149, no. 676.

206. TOBEY, NIELSEN AND ROWE 1984 [1986]. [Cf. PHILLIPS, IN PRESS.]

207. WARDEN, MADDIN, STECH AND MUHLY 1982; WARDEN 1985; and Warden in SIENA *CP,* 1985, 88–92, nos. 134–185 and 129–131, nos. 439–485. [See also, PHILLIPS 1989B.]

208. Inv. 70–68: WARDEN 1985, 52–53, no. 59 and figs. 15–16, pl. 7b; Warden in SIENA *CP,* 1985, 129, no. 451.

209. Inv. 78–27: WARDEN 1985, 83, no. 135; Warden in SIENA *CP,* 1985, 130, no. 467.

210. Talocchini in *POGGIO CIVITATE* 1970A–B, 18, nos. 8s–9s; SWADDLING AND CRADDOCK 1978.

211. Inv. 75–99: PHILLIPS 1978, 356–361, figs. 1–4; Phillips in AREZZO 1984, 136, no. 92; De Puma in SIENA *CP,* 1985, 93, no. 192.

212. Inv. 72–160: PHILLIPS 1978, 361–368, figs. 5–12; Phillips in AREZZO 1984, 136, no. 93; De Puma in SIENA *CP,* 1985, 93, no. 191.

213. Inv. 71–618 and 71–669: DE PUMA 1981 [1984], 86–87, pl. 26, figs. 3–4; De Puma in AREZZO 1984, 135, nos. 90–91; De Puma in SIENA *CP,* 1985, 93, nos. 186–187.

214. Inv. 71–722: DE PUMA 1981 [1984], 79–80, no. 2; De Puma in AREZZO 1984, 133, no. 87b; De Puma in SIENA *CP,* 1985, 93, no. 190b. Inv. 71–723: DE PUMA 1981 [1984], 80–81, no. 3; De Puma in AREZZO 1984, 133, no. 87c; De Puma in SIENA *CP,* 1985, 93, no. 190c.

215. DeMarinis in AREZZO 1984, 154, no. 136.

216. Inv. 71–282: PHILLIPS 1972, 254, pl. 53, figs. 17 and 18; Nielsen in AREZZO 1984, 133, no. 86; Nielsen in SIENA *CP,* 1985, 98, no. 215.

217. Inv. 71–92: PHILLIPS 1972, 253, pl. 51, figs. 13–14; Nielsen in AREZZO 1984, 127, no. 77; Nielsen in SIENA *CP,* 1985, 95, no. 199.

218. Inv. 71–280: Nielsen in AREZZO 1984, 126–127, no. 76; Nielsen in SIENA *CP,* 1985, 96, no. 201.

219. Inv. 71–198: PHILLIPS 1972, 253, pl. 51, figs. 15–16; Nielsen in AREZZO 1984, 126, no. 75; Nielsen in SIENA *CP,* 1985, 95, no. 200.

220. Inv. 71–500: NIELSEN AND PHILLIPS 1974, 274, pl. 58, figs. 19–20.

221. Inv. 71–102: PHILLIPS 1972, 253, pl. 52, figs. 11–12; Nielsen in AREZZO 1984, 130–131, no. 82; Nielsen in SIENA *CP,* 1985, 97, no. 209. Note the whittling strokes on the side of the face and the bold details of the mouth and eyes.

222. Inv. 71–100: PHILLIPS 1972, 254, pl. 53, fig. 21; CAPUTO 1972 [1974], 51; Nielsen in AREZZO 1984, 129–130, no. 81; Nielsen in SIENA *CP,* 1985, 98, no. 214. Nielsen and Caputo compare this small female figure with others from the Montagnola.

223. Inv. 71–101: Nielsen in AREZZO 1984, 131, no. 83; Nielsen in SIENA *CP,* 1985, 97, no. 210.

224. NIELSEN 1984A, 399.

PART III

225. Inv. 77–150: SIENA *CP,* 1985, 132, no. 489.

226. Inv. 79–88 and 79–173: SIENA *CP,* 1985, 78, nos. 52–53. [See also, PHILLIPS 1989A, 32, figs. 27–28, 29–30.]

227. *POGGIO CIVITATE* 1970A–B, 79–80. [See also, EDLUND-BERRY, "Ritual Destruction," IN PRESS.]

228. Norman Douglas *Old Calabria* (The Modern Library, New York 1928) 201–212.

Bibliography for Text and Notes

(Excavation reports are indicated with *, and primary studies with **.)

ANDRÉN 1940

A. Andrén, *Architectural Terracottas from Etrusco-Italic Temples*, Lund-Leipzig 1940 (*Acta Instituti Romani Regni Sueciae*, 6).

AREZZO 1984

Ministero dei Beni Culturali e Ambientali-Soprintendenza Archeologica della Toscana, *Cento preziosi etruschi: Catalogo della mostra dal 7 settembre 1984; centro affari e promozioni; dal 20 ottobre 1984: anfiteatro romano arezzo* ("Il Torchio," Florence 1984).

BARTOLONI ET AL. 1987

G. Bartoloni, F. Buranelli, V. D'Atri and A. De Santis, *Le urne a capanna rinvenute in Italia* (Tyrrhenica 1, Rome 1987).

BIANCHI BANDINELLI AND GIULIANO 1973B

Ranuccio Bianchi Bandinelli and Antonio Giuliano, *Les Étrusques et l'Italie avant Rome* (Gallinard, Paris 1973).

BOARDMAN 1971

J. Boardman, "A Southern View of Situla Art," in J. Boardman, M.A. Brown and T.G.E. Powell eds., *The European Community in Later Prehistory: Studies in Honour of C.F.C. Hawkes* (London 1971) 121–40.

BONFANTE 1981

L. Bonfante, *Out of Etruria: Etruscan Influence North and South* (*BAR Int. ser.* 103, 1981).

**BOULOUMIÉ 1978

Bernard Bouloumié, "Nouveaux instruments culinaires (?) en céramique de Murlo (Poggio Civitate)," *MélRome* 90:1 (1978) 113–131.

**BOULOUMIÉ-MARIQUE 1978

Antoinette Bouloumié-Marique, "La céramique commune de Murlo (Poggio Civitate)," *MélRome* 90:1 (1978) 52–112.

CAPUTO 1972 [1974]

Giacomo Caputo, "Cultura orientalizzante dell'Arno," in *Aspetti e problemi dell'Etruria interna: Atti dell'VIII Convegno Nazionale di Studi Etruschi ed Italici, Orvieto 27–30 giugno 1972* (Leo S. Olschki, Florence 1974) 19–66.

CRISTOFANI 1975

Mauro Cristofani, "Considerazioni su Poggio Civitate (Murlo, Siena)," *Prospettiva* 1 (1975) 9–17, figs. 1–15.

DELLA SETA 1918

A. Della Seta, *Museo di Villa Giulia* (Rome 1918).

**DE PUMA 1981 [1984]

Richard Daniel De Puma, "Etruscan Gold and Silver Jewelry from Poggio Civitate (Murlo)," *ArchCl* 23 (1981)

**EDLUND (GANTZ) 1972

Ingrid Edlund (Gantz), "The Seated Statue Akroteria from Poggio Civitate (Murlo)," *DialArch* 6 (1972) 167–235 figs. 1–44.

**EDLUND 1985A

Ingrid Edlund, "A Terracotta Head from Poggio Civitate (Murlo)," *OpRom* 15:3 (1985) 47–53, figs. 1–12

EDLUND 1987

Ingrid E.M. Edlund, *The Gods and the Place: Location and Function of Sanctuaries in the Countryside of Etruria and Magna Graecia (700–400 B.C.)*, Stockholm 1987 (*Acta Instituti Romani Regni Sueciae*, series in 4°, 43).

FABBRICOTTI 1977–1979 [1980]

Emanuela Fabbricotti, "Fregi fittili arcaici in Magna Grecia," *AttiMGrecia* NS 18–20 (1977–1979) [1980] 149–170, pls. 58–64.

**FULLERTON 1982

Mark D. Fullerton, "The Terracotta Sphinx Akroteria from Poggio Civitate (Murlo)," *RM* 89 (1982) 1–26, pls. 1–7.

**GANTZ 1971

Timothy Nolan Gantz, "Divine Triads on an Archaic Etruscan Frieze Plaque from Poggio Civitate (Murlo)," *StEtr* 39 (1971) 1–22, pls. 1–12.

**GANTZ 1974

Timothy Nolan Gantz, "The Procession Frieze from the Etruscan Sanctuary at Poggio Civitate," *RM* 81 (1974) 1–14, pls. 1–8.

MACINTOSH 1974

Jean MacIntosh, "Representations of Furniture on the Frieze Plaques from Poggio Civitate," *RM* 81 (1974) 15–40, pls. 9–20.

**MERITT 1970

Lucy Shoe Meritt, "Architectural Mouldings from Murlo," *StEtr* 38 (1970) 13–25, pls. 1–2.

**NEILS 1976

Jenifer Neils, "The Terracotta Gorgoneia of Poggio Civitate (Murlo)," *RM* 83 (1976) 1–29, pls. 1–10.

**NIELSEN 1984A

Erik O. Nielsen, "Lotus Chain Plaques from Poggio Civitate," in *Studi di antichità in onore di Guglielmo Maetzke* (Giorgio Bretschneider, Rome 1984) 397–399.

**NIELSEN 1985 [1989]

Erik O. Nielsen, "A New Lateral Sima from Poggio Civitate (Murlo)." Secondo Congresso Internazionale Etrusco, Atti vols. 1–3 (Giorgio Bretschneider, Rome 1989) 509–515, pls. I–III.

**NIELSEN 1987

Erik O. Nielsen, "Some Preliminary Thoughts on New and Old Terracottas," *OpRom* 16:5 (1987) 91–119, figs. 1–88.

*NIELSEN AND PHILLIPS 1974

Erik Nielsen and Kyle Meredith Phillips, Jr., "Bryn Mawr College Excavations in Tuscany, 1973," *AJA* 78 (1974) 265–278, pls. 55–59.

*NIELSEN AND PHILLIPS 1975

Erik Nielsen and Kyle Meredith Phillips, Jr., "Bryn Mawr College Excavations in Tuscany, 1974," *AJA* 79 (1975) 357–366, pls. 62–66.

*NIELSEN AND PHILLIPS 1976

Erik Nielsen and Kyle Meredith Phillips, Jr., "Poggio Civitate (Siena).—Gli scavi del Bryn Mawr College dal 1966 al 1974," *NSc* (ser. 8) 30 (1976) 113–147, figs. 1–38.

*NIELSEN AND PHILLIPS 1977A

E.O. Nielsen and K.M. Phillips, Jr., "Bryn Mawr College Excavations in Tuscany, 1975," *AJA* 81 (1977) 85–100, figs. 1–37.

*PHILLIPS 1966

Kyle Meredith Phillips, Jr., "Poggio Civitate (Siena).—Campagna di scavo 1966 del Bryn Mawr College in Toscana," *NSc* (ser. 8) 20 (1966) 5–17, figs. 1–21.

*PHILLIPS 1967A

Kyle Meredith Phillips, Jr., "Bryn Mawr College Excavations in Tuscany, 1966," *AJA* 71 (1967) 133–139, pls. 39–46.

*PHILLIPS 1967B

Kyle Meredith Phillips, Jr., "Scavi dell'università di Bryn Mawr a Poggio Civitate (Murlo, provincia di Siena)," *DialArch* 1 (1967) 245–247, figs. 39–41.

*PHILLIPS 1969A

Kyle Meredith Phillips, Jr., "Bryn Mawr College Excavations in Tuscany, 1968," *AJA* 73 (1969) 333–339, pls. 79–84.

*PHILLIPS 1969B

Kyle Meredith Phillips, Jr., "Poggio Civitate (Siena).—Campagna di scavi 1967 del Bryn Mawr College," *NSc* (ser. 8) 23 (1969) 38–50, figs. 1–18.

*PHILLIPS 1970A

Kyle Meredith Phillips, Jr., "Bryn Mawr College Excavations in Tuscany, 1969," *AJA* 74 (1970) 241–244, pls. 51–54.

*PHILLIPS 1971A

Kyle Meredith Phillips, Jr., "Bryn Mawr College Excavations in Tuscany, 1970," *AJA* 75 (1971) 257–261, pls. 57–62.

*PHILLIPS 1972

Kyle Meredith Phillips, Jr., "Bryn Mawr College Excavations in Tuscany, 1971," *AJA* 76 (1972) 249–255, pls. 49–54.

**PHILLIPS 1973B

Kyle Meredith Phillips, Jr., "Two Archaic Bronzes from Poggio Civitate," *OpRom* 9 (1973) 177–182, figs. 1–15.

**PHILLIPS 1978

Kyle Meredith Phillips, Jr., "Orientalizing Gem Stones from Poggio Civitate (Murlo, Siena)," *PP* Fasc. 182 (1978) 355–369, fig. 1–12.

PHILLIPS 1980

Kyle Meredith Phillips, Jr., "The Date of the Archaic Terracottas from Poggio Civitate," *PP* Fasc. 192 (=35) (1980) 202–206.

**PHILLIPS 1983

Kyle Meredith Phillips, Jr., "Terrecotte architettoniche con protomi di Leopardo da Poggio Civitate (Murlo, Siena)," *BdA* (ser. 6) 18 (1983) 1–24, figs. 1–55.

PHILLIPS 1984

Kyle Meredith Phillips, Jr., "Protective masks from Poggio Civitate and Chiusi," in *Studi di antichità in onore di Guglielmo Maetzke* (Giorgio Bretschneider, Rome 1984) 413–417, pls. I–II.

PHILLIPS 1985

Kyle Meredith Phillips, Jr., "Italic House Models and Etruscan Architectural Terracottas of the Seventh Century B.C. from Acquarossa and Poggio Civitate, Murlo," *AnalRom* 14 (1985) 7–16, figs. 1–12.

PHILLIPS 1986

Kyle Meredith Phillips, Jr., "Masks on a canopic Urn and an Etrusco-Corinthian perfume pot," in *Italian Iron Age Artefacts in the British Museum*, Papers of the Sixth British Museum Classical Colloquium, ed. Judith Swaddling (British Museum Publications, London 1986) 153–155.

POGGIO CIVITATE 1970A–B

Soprintendenza alle Antichità d'Etruria, *Poggio Civitate (Murlo, Siena): The Archaic Etruscan Sanctuary, Catalogue of the Exhibition, Florence-Siena, 1970* (Leo S. Olschki, Florence 1970). Text by Kyle Meredith Phillips, Jr. and Anna Talocchini. Translations by Luigi Donati and Lisa Mibach. Pp. 80, pls. 44.

RATHJE 1988

A. Rathje, "Manners and customs in central Italy in the Orientalizing period: influence form the Near East," *Acta Hyperborea* 1 (1988) 81–90.

RIDGWAY AND RIDGWAY 1984

Francesca R. Serra Ridgway and David Ridgway, review of Rystedt 1983, in *StEtr* 52 (1984) 544–554.

RIDGWAY AND RIDGWAY IN PRESS

D. and F.R. Ridgway, "Demaratus and the archaeologists," in DE PUMA AND SMALL EDS., IN PRESS [See p. 135].

RIESCH 1934

E. Riesch, "Rassegna degli Scavi e delle Scoperte nel suolo d'Etruria dal 1 Luglio 1933 al 30 Giugno 1934," *StEtr* 8 (1934) 335–337.

**ROOT 1973

Margaret Cool Root, "An Etruscan Horse Race from Poggio Civitate," *AJA* 77 (1973) 121–138, pls. 17–22.

**RYSTEDT 1983

Eva Rystedt, *Acquarossa Vol. IV. Early Etruscan Akroteria from Acquarossa and Poggio Civitate (Murlo)*, Stockholm 1983 (*Acta Instituti Romani Regni Sueciae*, series in 4°, 38:IV).

SIENA *CP*, 1985

Regione Toscana, *Case e palazzi d'Etruria*, ed. S. Stopponi (Electa, Milan, 1985).

**SMALL 1971

Jocelyn Penny Small, "The Banquet Frieze from Poggio Civitate (Murlo)," *StEtr* 39 (1971) 26–61, pls. 13–26.

STOCKHOLM 1972

Associazione Tuscia—Viterbo, *Gli Etruschi: Nuove ricerche e scoperte.* Mostra organizzata nel Museo Storico di Stato a Stoccolma dai seguenti Enti: L'Istituto Svedese di Studi Classici di Roma, Il Museo Mediterraneo di Stoccolma, Il Museo Storico di Stato di Stoccolma, La Soprintendenza alle Antichità dell'Etruria Meridionale. 6 novembre 1972–28 gennaio 1973 (Associazione Tuscia, Viterbo 1972).

SWADDLING AND CRADDOCK 1978

Judith Swaddling and Paul T. Craddock, "Etruscan Bronze Belt Clasps with Iron Inlay," *StEtr* 46 (1978) 47–55.

THUILLIER 1980

J.-P. Thuillier, "A propos des 'Triades Divines' de Poggio Civitate (Murlo)," in *Centre de recherches d'histoire et de philologie de la IVe Section de l'école pratique des hautes études, III Hautes études du monde gréco-romain, vol. 10, Recherches sur les religions de l'antiquité classique* (Droz, Geneva and Paris 1980), by Raymond Bloch and others, 385–394.

THUILLIER 1985

J.-P. Thuillier, *Les jeux athlétiques dans la civilisation étrusque* (Bibliotheque des écoles françaises d'Athènes et de Rome, 256, Rome 1985).

TOBEY, NIELSEN, AND ROWE 1984 [1986]

Mark H. Tobey, Erik O. Nielsen, and Marvin W. Rowe, "Elemental Analysis of Etruscan Ceramics from Murlo, Italy," *Proceedings of the 24th International Archaeometry Symposium*, ed. Jacqueline. S. Olin and M. James Blackman, (Smithsonian Institution Press, Washington, D.C. 1986) 115–127.

TORELLI 1980 [1983]

Mario Torelli, "*Polis* et 'palazzo'. Architettura, ideologia e artigianato greco in Etruria tra VII e VI sec. a.C.," in *Architecture et société de l'archaïsme grec à la fin de la république romaine* (Collection de l'école française de Rome, vol. 66, Rome 1980 [1983]) 471–492.

TORELLI 1985

M. Torelli, "Introduzione," in SIENA *CP*, 1985, 21–32.

**WARDEN 1977

P. Gregory Warden, "A Decorated Terracotta Stand from Poggio Civitate (Murlo)," *RM* 84 (1977) 199–210, pls. 101–110.

**WARDEN 1985

P. Gregory Warden, *The Metal Finds from Poggio Civitate (Murlo) 1966–1978* (Giorgio Bretschneider, Rome 1985).

WARDEN, MADDIN, STECH AND MUHLY 1982

P. Gregory Warden, Robert Maddin, Tamara Stech, James D. Muhly, "Copper and Iron Production at Poggio Civitate (Murlo): Analysis of Metalworking By-products from an Archaic Etruscan Site," *Expedition* 25 no. 1 (Fall 1982) 26–35, figs. 1–16.

**WINTER 1977

Nancy Ann Winter, "Architectural Terracottas with Human Heads from Poggio Civitate (Murlo)," *ArchCl* 29 (1977) 17–34, pls. 3–13.

WINTER 1978

Nancy Ann Winter, "Archaic Architectural Terracottas Decorated with Human Heads," *RM* 85 (1978) 27–58, pls. 7–22.

Concordance of Inventory Numbers

—

Numbers in italics refer to figures

An Annotated Bibliography on Poggio Civitate (Murlo)

The results of the excavations at Poggio Civitate have appeared in preliminary reports, published primarily in the *American Journal of Archaeology* and *Notizie degli Scavi*. But from the very first season, Kyle Phillips regarded it as part of his responsibility as an excavator to publish the material from the site as completely and as promptly as possible. Furthermore, if the excavations were to be considered a training ground for future archaeologists, he also wanted to include his students in the publications from the site.

The publication process began in the excavation storerooms at Murlo and Vescovado. As each object was cleaned and recorded, each catalogue entry was regarded as the initial step of study and publication. Students were encouraged to examine, analyze, and interpret every fragment, and the responsibility of accuracy in recording and description was shared by all.

This bibliography should be seen as a testimony to Kyle Phillips' philosophy of teaching his students, and of collaborating with colleagues from all over the world. As each of us began to study

groups of objects, and to present the results as notes, catalogue entries, or articles, it became clear that the bibliography of Murlo was going to be vast, complex, and distributed over most of the major archaeological publications. As a result, the site of Poggio Civitate is known by many, but it has become increasingly difficult for any one student or scholar to be familiar with everything published. Furthermore, it was Kyle Phillips' conviction that nothing could replace the actual handling, if not excavating, of each object to be studied. He therefore made a clear distinction in his mind, in the Murlo records, and in his own publications between primary and secondary studies. While the former might be preliminary, and could contain hypotheses which later might be disputed, the initial observations could never be replaced. The value of the secondary studies was to encourage scholars who knew the material primarily from photographs and the preliminary reports to present their interpretations, find new stylistic parallels, and to introduce material from other sites in Etruria or elsewhere.

The format of the bibliography as it now appears follows the guidelines

BIANCHI BANDINELLI AND GIULIANO 1973B

Ranuccio Bianchi Bandinelli and Antonio Giuliano, *Les étrusques et l'Italie avant Rome* (Gallinard, Paris 1973). [pp. 144–145, fig. 166 seated figures frieze (detail; drawing); pp. 194–196, fig. 226 sphinx, Inv. 68–500; fig. 227 head, Inv. 68–100; p. 374, fig. 446 'il cowboy', Inv. 67–411]

BLANCK 1970

Horst Blanck, "Murlo," in *AA* 85 (1970) 288–290. [brief summary; ills. of seated statue, Inv. 67–411; head, Inv. 68–200; antefix with human mask; see PHILLIPS 1984]

**BOULOUMIÉ 1972

Bernard Bouloumié, "Murlo (Poggio Civitate, Sienne): Céramique grossière locale. L'*instrumentum* culinaire," *MélRome* 84 (1972) 61–110. [interpretation and dating of utilitarian pottery of local impasto]

**BOULOUMIÉ 1978

Bernard Bouloumié, "Nouveaux instruments culinaires (?) en céramique de Murlo (Poggio Civitate)," *MélRome* 90:1 (1978) 113–131. [presentation of restored vases and interpretation of large vases with pierced holes]

**BOULOUMIÉ-MARIQUE 1978

Antoinette Bouloumié-Marique, "La céramique commune de Murlo (Poggio Civitate)," *MélRome* 90:1 (1978) 52–112. [study of local, non-decorated impasto and bucchero wares from the 1966–1969 seasons]

**CRISTOFANI AND PHILLIPS 1970

Mauro Cristofani and Kyle Meredith Phillips, Jr., "Ager Clusinus (Poggio Civitate, Murlo, Siena)," in *Rivista di epigrafia etrusca, StEtr* 38 (1970) 288–292. [letters and inscriptions on tiles and pottery]

**CRISTOFANI AND PHILLIPS 1971

Mauro Cristofani and Kyle M. Phillips, Jr., "Poggio Civitate: Etruscan Letters and Chronological Observations," *StEtr* 39 (1971) 409–430, pls. 84–92. [pottery, Inv. 66–95, 69–146, 69–92, 67–338, 67–68, 69–100, 66–112, 68–425, 67–377, 69–189, 68–372, 69–264, 69–250, 68–419, 66–151, 66–210, 66–17, 68–390a, 66–20, 68–431, 66–113; catalogue of letters]

**DAMGAARD ANDERSEN 1990

Helle Damgaard Andersen, "The Feline Waterspouts from the Lateral Sima of Poggio Civitate, Murlo," *OpRom* 18 (1990) 61–98.

**DE PUMA 1981 [1984]

Richard Daniel De Puma, "Etruscan Gold and Silver Jewelry from Poggio Civitate (Murlo)," *ArchCl* 23 (1981) [1984] 78–93, pls. 22–26. [publication of two miniature silver fibulae, Inv. 71–618; 71–669, a silver-backed gold fragment, Inv. 71–721, and reconstruction of five related gold fragments, Inv. 71–721bister; 71–222, 71–223, 71–224, as a fine bracelet, ca. 640–590 B.C.]

DONATI 1968

Luigi Donati, "Vasi di bucchero decorati con teste plastiche umane, zona di Chiusi," *StEtr* 36 (1968) 319–355, pls. 73–82. [p. 322, reference to *NSc* 1966, p. 10, fig. 10]

**DONATI 1971

Luigi Donati, "Frammento di bucchero con rappresentazione di cavalieri, da Poggio Civitate (Murlo)," *StEtr* 39 (1971) 307–311 pls. 62–63. [fragment Inv. 70–1]

**EDLUND (GANTZ) 1972

Ingrid Edlund (Gantz), "The Seated Statue Akroteria from Poggio Civitate (Murlo)," *DialArch* 6 (1972) 167–235 figs. 1–44. [identification of male and female seated statues as ridgepole akroteria probably depicting divine figures]

EDLUND (GANTZ) 1973

Ingrid Edlund (Gantz), "The Seated Statue Akroteria from Poggio Civitate (Murlo)," *AJA* 77 (1973) 213. [abstract of paper presented]

EDLUND (GANTZ) 1974

Ingrid Edlund (Gantz), "The Development of Etruscan Akroteria," Archaeological Institute of America, *Summaries,* 1974, 18–19. [abstract of paper presented]

EDLUND 1981 [1984]

Ingrid E.M. Edlund, "Sacred and secular: evidence of rural shrines and industry among Greeks and Etruscans," *Crossroads of the Mediterranean, Archaeologica Transatlantica II: Papers delivered at the International Conference held at Brown University,* ed. T. Hackens, Nancy D. Holloway and R. Ross Holloway (Louvain-la-Neuve and Providence, 1984) 277–290. [discussion of terracotta production at Poggio Civitate and mold of lateral sima head, Inv. 70–129, fig. 3 a–b]

**EDLUND 1985A

Ingrid Edlund, "A Terracotta Head from Poggio Civitate (Murlo)," *OpRom* 15:3 (1985) 47–53, figs. 1–12. [Inv. 68–100; tentatively identified as a bearded sphinx head]

EDLUND 1985B

Ingrid E.M. Edlund, "Man, Nature and the Gods: A Study of Rural Sanctuaries in Etruria and Magna Graecia from the Seventh to the Fourth Century B.C.," *Papers in Italian Archaeology IV. The Cambridge Conference,* Part iv Classical and Medieval Archaeology, ed. C. Malone and S. Stoddart, Oxford 1985 (British Archaeological Reports International Series 246), 21–32. [discussion of Murlo as a 'confederate' sanctuary]

EDLUND 1987

Ingrid E.M. Edlund, *The Gods and the Place: Location and Function of Sanctuaries in the Countryside of Etruria and Magna Graecia (700–400 B.C.),* Stockholm 1987 (*Acta Instituti Romani Regni Sueciae,* series in 4°, 43). [pp. 64, 85, 86, 87, 90–92, 129, 136, 137, 138, 139, 143, 144, 145, fig. 8, ill. 12, discussion of Poggio Civitate as a 'political sanctuary']

EDLUND-BERRY 1989A

"Religion, Politics and Archaeology: Evidence for the Shrine of Voltumna and Other Political Sanctuaries," *AJA* 93 (1989) 257–258. [abstract of paper presented]

EDLUND-BERRY 1989B

"Four Terracotta Heads from Poggio Civitate (Murlo); Towards a Definition of the 'Murlo Style'," *OpRom* 17:3 (1989) 21–32. [discussion of two lateral sima heads, Inv. nos. 68–84 and 68–32, a human head fragment, Inv. 71–167, and a human head vase fragment, Inv. 68–160]

EDLUND-BERRY 1991

Ingrid E.M. Edlund-Berry, "Power and Religion: How Social Change Affected the Emergence and Collapse of Power Structures in Central Italy." *Papers of the Fourth Conference of Italian Archaeology. The Archaeology of Power, part 2* (London 1991), 161–172.

EDLUND-BERRY 1992

Ingrid E.M. Edlund-Berry, *The Seated and Standing Statue Akroteria from Poggio Civitate (Murlo)* (Giorgio Bretschneider, Rome 1992).

FABBRICOTTI 1977–1979 [1980]

Emanuela Fabbricotti, "Fregi fittili arcaici in Magna Grecia," *AttiMGrecia* NS 18–20 (1977–1979) [1980] 149–170, pls. 58–64. [comparison between frieze plaques from Poggio Civitate and examples from Serra di Vaglio, Metaponto, and S. Biagio]

**FULLERTON 1982

Mark D. Fullerton, "The Terracotta Sphinx Akroteria from Poggio Civitate (Murlo)," *RM* 89 (1982) 1–26, pls. 1–7. [Inv. 68–500 and other sphinx fragments]

**GANTZ 1971

Timothy Nolan Gantz, "Divine Triads on an Archaic Etruscan Frieze Plaque from Poggio Civitate (Murlo)," *StEtr* 39 (1971) 1–22, pls. 1–12. [tentative interpretation of seated figures frieze as representing two divine triads]

**GANTZ 1974

Timothy Nolan Gantz, "The Procession Frieze from the Etruscan Sanctuary at Poggio Civitate," *RM* 81 (1974) 1–14, pls. 1–8. [interpretation of frieze as representing procession of noblemen approaching the gods depicted on the seated figures frieze]

GANTZ 1975

Timothy Nolan Gantz, "Terracotta Figured Friezes from the Workshop of Vulca," *OpRom* 10 (1974–1975) 1–9. [p. 2 n. 10 seated figures frieze]

MACINTOSH 1974

Jean MacIntosh, "Representations of Furniture on the Frieze Plaques from Poggio Civitate," *RM* 81 (1974) 15–40, pls. 9–20. [detailed analysis of Greek, Oriental, and Etruscan features depicted on frieze plaques]

MASSA-PAIRAULT 1986

Françoise-Hélène Massa-Pairault, "Les jeux équestres de Murlo; Représentation et société," *Ktema* 11 (1986) 179–187.

MELIS AND RATHJE 1984

Francesca Melis and Annette Rathje, "Considerazioni sullo studio dell'architettura domestica arcaica," *Archeologia laziale* 6 (1984) (=Quaderni del centro di studio per l'archeologia etrusco-italica, 8) 382–395 [p. 383 discussion of Poggio Civitate as a domestic structure; p. 395, n. 55]

**MERITT 1970

Lucy Shoe Meritt, "Architectural Mouldings from Murlo," *StEtr* 38 (1970) 13–25, pls. 1–2. [analysis of profiles of sima and frieze plaques; trophy on horserace frieze]

**NEILS 1976

Jenifer Neils, "The Terracotta Gorgoneia of Poggio Civitate (Murlo)," *RM* 83 (1976) 1–29, pls. 1–10. [catalogue and discussion]

NIELSEN 1981 [1984]A

Erik O. Nielsen, "Some Observations on Early Etruria," *Crossroads of the Mediterranean, Archaeologica Transatlantica II: Papers delivered at the International Conference held at Brown University*, ed. T. Hackens, Nancy D. Holloway and R. Ross Holloway (Louvain-la-Neuve and Providence, 1984) 255–259. [brief summary and bibliographical overview]

**NIELSEN 1981 [1984]B

Erik O. Nielsen, "Speculations on an Ivory Workshop of the Orientalizing Period," *Crossroads of the Mediterranean, Archaeologica Transatlantica II: Papers delivered at the International Conference held at Brown University*, ed. T. Hackens, Nancy D. Holloway and R. Ross Holloway (Louvain-la-Neuve and Providence, 1984) 333–348, figs. 1–23. [bone and ivory fragments from the 'Lower Building']

*NIELSEN 1981C

Erik O. Nielsen, "Recent Excavations at Poggio Civitate (Murlo)," *AJA* 85 (1981) 209. [abstract of paper presented]

*NIELSEN 1983 [1991]

Erik O. Nielsen, "Excavations at Poggio Civitate," *Studi e Materiali* 6 (1983) [1991] 245–259.

**NIELSEN 1984A

Erik O. Nielsen, "Lotus Chain Plaques from Poggio Civitate," in *Studi di antichità in onore di Guglielmo Maetzke* (Giorgio Bretschneider, Rome 1984) 397–399. [discussion of cutting techniques of bone and existence of workshop at Poggio Civitate; Inv. 71–259, 71–653/654/655/656/657/658, 71–860, 77–10]

NIELSEN 1984B

Erik O. Nielsen, review of P.J. Riis 1981, in *ArchNews* 13 (1984) 48–49. [discussion of the chronology of the buildings at Poggio Civitate]

**NIELSEN 1985 [1989]

Erik O. Nielsen, "A New Lateral Sima from Poggio Civitate (Murlo)." *Secondo Congresso Internazionale Etrusco, Atti* vols. 1–3 (Giorgio Bretschneider, Rome 1989) 509–515, pls. I–III.

**NIELSEN 1987

Erik O. Nielsen, "Some Preliminary Thoughts on New and Old Terracottas," *OpRom* 16:5 (1987) 91–119, figs. 1–88. [evidence for earliest terracotta production at Poggio Civitate]

*NIELSEN 1989

Erik O. Nielsen, "Excavations at Poggio Civitate, Italy," *AJA* 93 (1989) 258. [abstract of paper presented]

*NIELSEN AND PHILLIPS 1974

Erik Nielsen and Kyle Meredith Phillips, Jr., "Bryn Mawr College Excavations in Tuscany, 1973," *AJA* 78 (1974) 265–278, pls. 55–59.

*NIELSEN AND PHILLIPS 1975

Erik Nielsen and Kyle Meredith Phillips, Jr., "Bryn Mawr College Excavations in Tuscany, 1974," *AJA* 79 (1975) 357–366, pls. 62–66.

*NIELSEN AND PHILLIPS 1976

Erik Nielsen and Kyle Meredith Phillips, Jr., "Poggio Civitate (Siena). — Gli scavi del Bryn Mawr College dal 1966 al 1974," *NSc* (ser. 8) 30 (1976) 113–147, figs. 1–38.

*NIELSEN AND PHILLIPS 1977A

Erik Nielsen and Kyle Meredith Phillips, Jr., "Bryn Mawr College Excavations in Tuscany, 1975," *AJA* 81 (1977) 85–100, figs. 1–37.

*NIELSEN AND PHILLIPS 1977B

Erik O. Nielsen and Kyle M. Phillips, Jr., "Murlo (Siena)," *StEtr* 45 (1977) 464–465, pl. 71 (in Scavi e scoperte).

*NIELSEN AND PHILLIPS 1983 [1986]

Erik O. Nielsen and Kyle M. Phillips, Jr., "Poggio Civitate (Siena). The Excavations at Murlo in 1976–1978," *NSc* (ser. 8) 37 (1983) [1986] 5–24, figs. 1–16.

*PHILLIPS 1966

Kyle Meredith Phillips, Jr., "Poggio Civitate (Siena). — Campagna di scavo 1966 del Bryn Mawr College in Toscana," *NSc* (ser. 8) 20 (1966) 5–17, figs. 1–21.

*PHILLIPS 1967A

Kyle Meredith Phillips, Jr., "Bryn Mawr College Excavations in Tuscany, 1966," *AJA* 71 (1967) 133–139, pls. 39–46.

*PHILLIPS 1967B

Kyle Meredith Phillips, Jr., "Scavi dell'università di Bryn Mawr a Poggio Civitate (Murlo, provincia di Siena)," *DialArch* 1 (1967) 245–247, figs. 39–41.

*PHILLIPS 1968A

Kyle Meredith Phillips, Jr. "Bryn Mawr College Excavations in Tuscany, 1967," *AJA* 72 (1968) 121–124, pls. 45–52.

*PHILLIPS 1968B

Kyle Meredith Phillips, Jr., "Poggio Civitate," *Archaeology* 21:4 (1968) 252–261 and color cover.

*PHILLIPS 1968C

Kyle Meredith Phillips, Jr., "Scavi del Bryn Mawr College in Toscana durante l'estate 1967," *DialArch* 2 (1968) 104–106, figs. 1–2.

*PHILLIPS 1969A

Kyle Meredith Phillips, Jr., "Bryn Mawr College Excavations in Tuscany, 1968," *AJA* 73 (1969) 333–339, pls. 79–84.

*PHILLIPS 1969B

Kyle Meredith Phillips, Jr.,
"Poggio Civitate (Siena). —
Campagna di scavi 1967 del
Bryn Mawr College," *NSc* (ser.
8) 23 (1969) 38–50, figs. 1–18.

*PHILLIPS 1970A

Kyle Meredith Phillips, Jr.,
"Bryn Mawr College Excavations in Tuscany, 1969," *AJA* 74
(1970) 241–244, pls. 51–54.

PHILLIPS 1970B

Kyle Meredith Phillips, Jr.,
"Grant No. 872. — Johnson
Fund (1968), $ 1,000. Bryn
Mawr College excavations at
Poggio Civitate," *Year Book of
the American Philosophical Society*
1970, 675–676.

*PHILLIPS 1971A

Kyle Meredith Phillips, Jr.,
"Bryn Mawr College Excavations in Tuscany, 1970," *AJA* 75
(1971) 257–261, pls. 57–62.

PHILLIPS 1971B

Kyle Meredith Phillips, Jr.,
"Grant No. 5546 — Penrose
Fund (1970), $ 1,000. Bryn
Mawr College excavations
at Poggio Civitate: fifth campaign, summer of 1970,"
*Year Book of The American
Philosophical Society* 1971,
655–656.

*PHILLIPS 1972

Kyle Meredith Phillips, Jr.,
"Bryn Mawr College Excavations in Tuscany, 1971," *AJA* 76
(1972) 249–255, pls. 49–54.

*PHILLIPS 1973A

Kyle Meredith Phillips, Jr.,
"Bryn Mawr College
Excavations in Tuscany, 1972,"
AJA 77 (1973) 319–326, pls.
53–58.

**PHILLIPS 1973B

Kyle Meredith Phillips, Jr.,
"Two Archaic Bronzes from
Poggio Civitate," *OpRom* 9
(1973) 177–182, figs. 1–15.
[wrestler, Inv. 71–105; umpire,
Inv. 71–106]

PHILLIPS 1973C

Kyle Meredith Phillips, Jr., s.v.
Poggio Civitate in *EAA,*
Supplemento 1970 (Rome
1973), 629–632 figs. 635–638.
[summary of excavations and
finds; fig. 635 seated figures
frieze, Inv. 68–264; fig. 636
lateral sima head, Inv. 67–20;
fig. 637 gorgon antefix, Inv.
68–68; fig. 638 feline head,
Inv. 66–229]

PHILLIPS 1974A

Kyle Meredith Phillips, Jr.,
"Poggio Civitate (Murlo,
Siena) 1966–1972," in *Aspetti e
problemi dell'Etruria interna: Atti
dell'VIII Convegno Nazionale di
Studi Etruschi ed Italici, Orvieto,
27–30 giugno 1972* (Leo S.
Olschki, Florence 1974)
141–146. [summary of excavations]

PHILLIPS 1974B

Kyle Meredith Phillips, Jr.,
"The Murlo Museum in
Siena," *Archaeology* 27 (1974)
133.

PHILLIPS 1976

Kyle Meredith Phillips, Jr., "Poggio Civitate (Murlo)," *The Princeton Encyclopaedia of Classical Sites*, ed. Richard Stillwell (Princeton, N.J. 1976) 719.

**PHILLIPS 1978

Kyle Meredith Phillips, Jr., "Orientalizing Gem Stones from Poggio Civitate (Murlo, Siena)," *PP* Fasc. 182 (1978) 355–369, fig. 1–12. [Inv. 75–99 and 72–160]

PHILLIPS 1980

Kyle Meredith Phillips, Jr., "The Date of the Archaic Terracottas from Poggio Civitate," *PP* Fasc. 192 (=35) (1980) 202–206. [summary of dating evidence from pottery]

**PHILLIPS 1983

Kyle Meredith Phillips, Jr., "Terrecotte architettoniche con protomi di Leopardo da Poggio Civitate (Murlo, Siena)," *BdA* (ser. 6) 18 (1983) 1–24, figs. 1–55. [classification of 'leopard' protomes]

PHILLIPS 1984

Kyle Meredith Phillips, Jr., "Protective masks from Poggio Civitate and Chiusi," in *Studi di antichità in onore di Guglielmo Maetzke* (Giorgio Bretschneider, Rome 1984) 413–417, pls. I–II. [discussion of antefix with human mask, Inv. 68–196]

PHILLIPS 1985

Kyle Meredith Phillips, Jr., "Italic House Models and Etruscan Architectural Terracottas of the Seventh Century B.C. from Acquarossa and Poggio Civitate, Murlo," *AnalRom* 14 (1985) 7–16, figs. 1–12. [discussion of horse-and-rider akroterion, fragment, Inv. 68–477; horse-and-rider akroterion, Inv. 69–282, figs. 7–8; horse-and-rider akroterion, fragment, Inv. 68–474, figs. 9–10]

PHILLIPS 1986

Kyle Meredith Phillips, Jr., "Masks on a canopic Urn and an Etrusco-Corinthian perfume pot," in *Italian Iron Age Artefacts in the British Museum*, Papers of the Sixth British Museum Classical Colloquium, ed. Judith Swaddling (British Museum Publications, London 1986) 153–155 [fig. 5 antefix with human mask, Inv. 68–196]

PHILLIPS 1989A

Kyle Meredith Phillips, Jr., "Greek Objects at Poggio Civitate, Murlo," *AnalRom* 17–18 (1989) 29–42. [discussion of imported Greek pottery and group of bronze wrestlers, for which see also PHILLIPS 1973B and WARDEN 1982]

PHILLIPS 1989B

Kyle Meredith Phillips, Jr., "Notes from Berlin on a Bronze Owl," *OpRom* 17:8 (1989) 97–122. [discussion of Inv. 79–176]

**PHILLIPS 1990

Kyle Meredith Phillips, Jr., "The Lateral Sima from Poggio Civitate (Murlo): Notes on Early Etruscan Craftsmanship." *OpRom* 18 (1990) 139–157.

RASMUSSEN 1986

Tom Rasmussen, "Archaeology in Etruria, 1980–1985," in *AR* 32 (1986) 102–122. [p. 119, fig. 26 plan of building phases]

RATHJE 1982

Annette Rathje, "Hvor graves der i dag," in *Etruskernes verden: Livet og døden hos et oldtidsfolk i Italien* (National Museum, Copenhagen, 1982). [pp. 107–110; ill. of panther head]

RATHJE 1983

Annette Rathje, "A Banquet Service from the Latin City of Ficana," *AnalRom* 12 (1983) 7–29. [p. 24 banquet frieze; p. 26]

RATHJE 1988

Annette Rathje, "Manners and Customs in Central Italy in the Orientalizing Period: Influence from the Near East," *Acta Hyperborea* 1 (1988) 81–90. [pp. 87–88 and figs. 10a–b banquet frieze from Poggio Civitate]

RATHJE 1989

Annette Rathje, "Alcune considerazioni sulle lastre da Poggio Civitate con figure femminili," in *Le donne in Etruria*, ed. Antonia Rallo (Laterza, Bari 1989). [pp. 75–84, pls. xxx–xxxii]

RIDGWAY 1974

David Ridgway, "Archaeology in Central Italy and Etruria, 1968–1973," in *AR* no. 20 (1974) 42–59. [pp. 56–57 summary; ills. of head, Inv. 68–200, and frieze plaques]

RIESCH 1934

E. Riesch, "Rassegna degli Scavi e delle Scoperte nel suolo d'Etruria dal 1 Luglio 1933 al 30 Giugno 1934," *StEtr* 8 (1934) 335–337. [p. 337 helmet and spear point from Murlo]

**ROOT 1973

Margaret Cool Root, "An Etruscan Horse Race from Poggio Civitate," *AJA* 77 (1973) 121–138, pls. 17–22. [stylistic analysis]

**RYSTEDT 1983

Eva Rystedt, *Acquarossa Vol. IV. Early Etruscan Akroteria from Acquarossa and Poggio Civitate (Murlo)*, Stockholm 1983 (*Acta Instituti Romani Regni Sueciae*, series in 4°, 38:IV). [analysis of cut-out akroteria from both sites and of relief-modeled ones from Poggio Civitate; a definition of their place within the early terracotta production of Etruria and their relationship to early Greek akroteria] [reviews by DOWNEY 1986; SERRA RIDGWAY AND RIDGWAY 1984; TORELLI 1986]

RYSTEDT 1984

Eva Rystedt, "Architectural Terracotta as Aristocratic Display. The case of seventh-century Poggio Civitate (Murlo)," *Opus* 3:2 (1984) 367–376, figs. 1–2. [aristocratic connections of the architectural terracottas decorating the 7th-century building complex at Poggio Civitate, based on an analysis of the cut-out akroteria]

SCHEFFER 1976

Charlotte Scheffer, "Cooking Stands and Some Possibly Related Objects from Acquarossa. A Preliminary Report," *OpRom* 11 (1976) 39–52. [pp. 49–50 references to BOULOUMIÉ 1972]

SCHEFFER 1981

Charlotte Scheffer, *Acquarossa Vol. II:1. Cooking and Cooking Stands in Italy 1400–400 B.C.,* Stockholm 1981 (*Acta Instituti Romani Regni Sueciae,* series in 4°, 38:II.1). [passim, references to BOULOUMIÉ 1972] [reviews by RIDGWAY 1983; TORELLI 1986]

SCHEFFER 1985

Charlotte Scheffer, "Was there a Garden at Poggio Civitate?" *OpRom*, 15:10 (1985) 105–108 [discussion of vase Inv. 73–137; previously interpreted by BOULOUMIÉ 1972, 1978 as a brazier or lantern]

SCHEFFER 1987

"Forni e fornelli etruschi in età arcaica," in *ALIMENTAZIONE* 1987, 97–105. [pp. 99, 101 braziers and 'cooking bells'; references to BOULOUMIÉ 1972, 1978, and SIENA *CP*, 1985]

SCHEFFER 1990

Charlotte Scheffer, "Domus Regiae—a Greek Tradition?," *OpAth* 18 (1990) 185–191. [p. 189]

**SMALL 1971

Jocelyn Penny Small, "The Banquet Frieze from Poggio Civitate (Murlo)," *StEtr* 39 (1971) 26–61, pls. 13–26. [unusual orientation of the heads of the klinai on the left, among other factors, support a date in the second quarter of the sixth century B.C.]

TALOCCHINI 1949

Anna Talocchini, "Forma Etruriae. Carta archeologica d'Italia al 100.000," *StEtr* 20 (1949) 219–220. [p. 220 finds from Murlo]

TOBEY, NIELSEN, AND ROWE 1984 [1986]

Mark H. Tobey, Erik O. Nielsen, and Marvin W. Rowe, "Elemental Analysis of Etruscan Ceramics from Murlo, Italy," *Proceedings of the 24th International Archaeometry Symposium,* ed. Jacqueline. S. Olin and M. James Blackman, (Smithsonian Institution Press, Washington, D.C. 1986) 115–127.

VALENTINI 1969

Giovanna Valentini, "Il motivo della Potnia Theron sui vasi di bucchero," *StEtr* 37 (1969) 413–442, pls. 105–110. [p. 428 no. 63 handle fragment, Inv. 66–112]

**VALENTINI 1970

Giovanna Valentini, "Un nuovo tipo di Potnia Theron sui vasi di bucchero," *StEtr* 38 (1970) 361, pl. 50. [bucchero fragments, Inv. 68–433 and Inv. 68–435]

**WARDEN 1977

P. Gregory Warden, "A Decorated Terracotta Stand from Poggio Civitate (Murlo)," *RM* 84 (1977) 199–210, pls. 101–110. [Inv. 67–450]

**WARDEN 1979

P. Gregory Warden, "An Etruscan Bronze Group from Poggio Civitiate (Murlo)." *AJA* 84 (1980) 238. [abstract of paper presented]

**WARDEN 1982

P. Gregory Warden, "An Etruscan Bronze Group," *AJA* 86 (1982) 233–238, pls. 33–35. [wrestler, Inv. 71–105; umpire, Inv. 71–106]

**WARDEN 1983

P. Gregory Warden, "Bullae, Roman Custom and Italic Tradition," *OpRom* 14 (1983) 69–75. [discussion of bronze bullae, Inv. 68–453, fig. 1, and Inv. 71–120]

**WARDEN 1985

P. Gregory Warden, *The Metal Finds from Poggio Civitate (Murlo) 1966–1978* (Giorgio Bretschneider, Rome 1985). [catalogue and analysis] [review by DE RUYT 1987]

WARDEN, MADDIN, STECH AND MUHLY 1982

P. Gregory Warden, Robert Maddin, Tamara Stech, James D. Muhly, "Copper and Iron Production at Poggio Civitate (Murlo): Analysis of Metal-working By-products from an Archaic Etruscan Site," *Expedition* 25 no. 1 (Fall 1982) 26–35, figs. 1–16. [fig. 4 belt buckle; fig. 11 rein ring, Inv. 71–706; fig. 12 bronze wrestler, Inv. 71–105; fig. 13 iron adze, Inv. 71–97; fig. 14 bronze tack, Inv. 71–629; fig. 15 furniture attachment, Inv. 67–56; fig. 16 bronze bulla, Inv. 71–120]

WARDEN, MADDIN, STECH AND MUHLY 1983 [1991]

P. Gregory Warden, Robert Maddin, Tamara Stech, and James D. Muhly, "Analyses of Metalworking By-Products from Poggio Civitate (Murlo)," in *Studi e Materiali* 6 (1983) [1991] 151–156.

WIKANDER 1972

Örjan Wikander, "Etruscan roofing-tiles from Acquarossa. A preliminary report," *OpRom* 8 (1972) 17–28. [p. 19, n. 21 ridge tiles]

WIKANDER 1981

Örjan Wikander, "Architectural Terracottas from San Giovenale," *OpRom* 13 (1981) 69–89. [p. 82 ridge tiles]

WIKANDER 1986

Örjan Wikander, *Acquarossa Vol. VI. The Roof-tiles. Part 1. Catalogue and Architectural Context*, Stockholm 1986 (*Acta Instituti Romani Regni Sueciae*, series in 4°, 38:VI,1). [p. 13, n. 5 finds of roof tiles]

WIKANDER 1988

Örjan Wikander, "Ancient Roof-tiles—use and function," *OpAth* 17:15 (1988) 203–216. [p. 205, n. 19; p. 206, nn. 24, 27; p. 207, n. 43; p. 208, n. 53; p. 213, L1, n. 86; p. 213, L3, n. 88; p. 215, n. 115; p. 216, n. 132; fig. 5:L1 ridgepole tile, Inv. 70–344]

CH. AND Ö. WIKANDER 1990

Charlotte and Örjan Wikander, "The Early Monumental Complex at Acquarossa. A preliminary report." *OpRom* 18 (1990) 189–205. [p. 205 date of Orientalizaing complex]

**WINTER 1977

Nancy Ann Winter, "Architectural Terracottas with Human Heads from Poggio Civitate (Murlo)," *ArchCl* 29 (1977) 17–34, pls. 3–13. [catalogue and analysis]

WINTER 1978

Nancy Ann Winter, "Archaic Architectural Terracottas Decorated with Human Heads," *RM* 85 (1978) 27–58, pls. 7–22. [pp. 31, 34–35, 50, 54 n. 95, 55; pl. 8 figs. 1–2, antefix with human mask, Inv. 68–196; pl. 10 figs. 1–2 lateral sima head, Inv. 68–504]

II. SECONDARY STUDIES

The secondary studies derive primarily from published material rather than from first hand inspection of the material. The reference may be to only one piece and may be listed only in a note. Included are also reviews of the primary studies listed in section I.

ALFÖLDI 1976

Andreas Alföldi, *Römische Frühgeschichte* (Winter, Heidelberg 1976). [pp. 129–130 discussion of seated figures frieze, with reference to GANTZ 1971; does not accept interpretation of Ceres, Liber, and Libera; p. 167, n. 108 reference to horserace frieze plaque with pointed caps]

ANDRÉN 1971

Arvid Andrén, "Lectiones Boëthianae I: Osservazioni sulle terrecotte architettoniche etrusco-italiche," *OpRom* 8 (1971) 1–16, pls. 40. [passim in text; fig. 40 horserace frieze; fig. 41 drawing of horserace frieze; fig. 42 fragment of banquet frieze; fig. 43 drawing of banquet frieze; fig. 44 seated figures frieze; fig. 45 drawing of seated figures frieze; figs. 46–48 fragments of procession frieze; fig. 49 drawing of procession frieze]

APRILE 1979

Renato Aprile, *Die Etrusker* (Verlag Freies Geistesleben, Stuttgart 1979). [pp. 81, 83, 143 importance of Poggio Civitate]

BANTI 1969

Luisa Banti, *Il mondo degli Etruschi* (Biblioteca di Storia Patria, Rome 1969). [p. 223]

BANTI 1973

Luisa Banti, *Etruscan Cities and their Culture* (Batsford, London 1973). Translated by Erika Bizzari. [p. 143 reference to belt-buckles; p. 174 monumental building described as 'place of worship']

BARTOLONI AND GROTTANELLI 1984

Gilda Bartoloni and Cristiano Grottanelli, " I carri a due ruote nelle tombe femminili del Lazio e dell'Etruria," *Opus* 3:2 (1984) 383–410. [pp. 386–387 horses at Poggio Civitate; procession frieze, fig. 3A, from GANTZ 1974]

BATINI AND BATINI PRESENTI 1985

Giorgio Batini and Maria Novella Batini Presenti, *Etruschi curiosi* (Bonecchi, Florence 1985). [pp. 184–185 reference to the 'dumps' (deposits) of terracottas and their relation to the sacred building ('edificio sacro')]

BEIJER 1987

Arnold J. Beijer, "Scavi a Le Ferriere ("Satricum") 1983–1985," *Archeologia laziale* 8 (1987) 278–284 (=*Quaderni del centro di studio per l'archeologia etrusco-italica*, 14). [p. 281 Poggio Civitate]

BERGQUIST 1973

Birgitta Bergquist, "Was there A Formal Dining-Room on the Acropolis of Acquarossa?" *OpRom* 9 (1973) 21–34. [p. 26, n. 13 comparison between peristyle building at Troizen, dated to 300 or early 3rd century B.C., and Poggio Civitate]

BERNARDINI 1982

Enzo Bernardini, *Toscana antica* (Sagep, Genova 1982). [pp. 97, 170–172, 216; fig. 153 site (color plate of present-day view); fig. 154 'il cowboy', Inv. 67–411; fig. 155 reconstruction of roof; fig. 156 sphinx, Inv. 68–500; fig. 157 terracotta stand, Inv. 67–450; fig. 165 plan; fig. 166 banquet frieze]

BOETTI 1980

Giovanni Boetti, *Suavis locus ille Sovicille* (Centrooffset, Siena 1980). [p. 28 and p. 30, n. 8]

BOITANI, CATALDI, PASQUINUCCI 1973

Francesca Boitani, Maria Cataldi, Marinella Pasquinucci, *Le città etrusche* (Mondadori, Milan 1973; English ed. *Etruscan Cities,* Cassell, London 1975). [p. 85 description and plan]

BOJESEN, CHRISTIANSEN, BRUUN, AND YDE 1983

Christian Bo Bojesen, Hanne Christiansen, Niels W. Bruun, Inger Yde, *Etruskerne* (Systime, Herning 1983). [pp. 70–71; fig. 50 plan; fig. 51 'il cowboy', Inv. 67–411]

BONAMICI 1974

Marisa Bonamici, *I buccheri con figurazioni graffite* (Istituto di Studi Etruschi ed Italici. Biblioteca di 'Studi Etruschi' Vol. 8, Florence 1974). [p. 169, n. 319 reference to terracotta stand, Inv. 67–450]

BONFANTE 1970

Larissa Bonfante Warren, "Roman Triumphs and Etruscan Kings: The Latin Word *Triumphus,*" *JRS* 60 (1970) 49–66. [n. 69 does not accept seated figures frieze as divine triads]

BONFANTE 1975

Larissa Bonfante, *Etruscan Dress* (The Johns Hopkins University Press, Baltimore 1975). [pp. 3, 35, 62, 69, 88, 118, 124, 131–132, 135; fig. 72 procession and seated figures friezes; fig. 121 'il cowboy', Inv. 67–411]

BONFANTE 1976

Larissa Bonfante, "Etruscan Influence in Northern Italy," *ArchNews* 5 (1976) 93–106. [text, passim; fig. 8 seated figures frieze; fig. 9 procession frieze; fig. 10 'il cowboy', Inv. 67–411; fig. 11 horserace frieze]

BONFANTE 1979A

Larissa Bonfante, "I popoli delle situle: Una civiltà pro-tourbana," *DialArch*, Nuova serie, 1 part 2 (1979) 73–94. [pp. 75, 79, 82, 83, 84, 85, 88, 90, 91; fig. 3 'il cowboy', Inv. 67–411; fig. 14 seated figures frieze; fig. 15 procession frieze; fig. 16 banquet frieze, fig. 17 horserace frieze]

BONFANTE 1979B

Larissa Bonfante, "I 'Popoli delle Situle' e l'arte etrusco," *Prospettiva* 17 (1979) 31–36. [p. 32 'cowboy' hat and pointed shoes on seated statues; comparison with situla Benvenuti]

BONFANTE 1981

Larissa Bonfante, *Out of Etruria: Etruscan Influence North and South,* BAR International Series 103 (Oxford 1981). [text, passim; fig. 28 'il cowboy', Inv. 67–411; figs. 31–34 frieze plaques; fig. 35 plan]

BONFANTE 1986

Larissa Bonfante, ed., *Etruscan Life and Afterlife* (Wayne State University Press, Detroit 1986). [text, passim; fig. IV 52–55 frieze plaques; IV 56a (not b!) gorgon; IV 57 'il cowboy', Inv. 67–411; fig. V 33 plan]

BONFANTE AND BONFANTE 1983

Giuliano Bonfante and Larissa Bonfante, *The Etruscan Language* (New York University Press, New York 1983). [p. 28 territory of Chiusi]

BONNIN 1973

J. Bonnin, "Les hydrauliciens étrusques: Des precurseurs?," *La houille blanche* 8 (1973) 641–649. [p. 645 terracotta drain pipes from Poggio Civitate; fig. 12 drawing]

BOSI 1985

Roberto Bosi, *Itinerari in terra d'Etruria* (Nardini, Florence 1985). [p. 224 line drawings of banquet, seated figures, and procession frieze; pp. 225–228 text; p. 234 sphinx, Inv. 68–500]

BRENDEL 1978

Otto J. Brendel, *Etruscan Art* (The Pelican History of Art, Penguin Books, Harmondworth, Eng. and New York 1978). [p. 455, n. 4 terracotta statues; p. 457, n. 13 terracotta frieze plaques]

BROWN 1974

A.C. Brown, "Etrusco-Italic Architectural Terra-cottas in the Ashmolean Museum, Oxford," *AR* 20 (1974) 60–65. [p. 65 lion-head waterspouts]

BROWN 1975

Frank E. Brown, "La protostoria della Regia," *RendPontAtt* 47 (1974–1975) 15–36. [pp. 34–35 discussion of Acquarossa and Poggio Civitate]

BUZZI 1984

Giancarlo Buzzi, *Guida alla Civiltà etrusca* (Mondadori, Milan 1984). [pp. 175–177 general discussion; p. 176 plan of building]

CAMPOREALE 1973

Giovannangelo Camporeale, "Vasi plastici di bucchero pesante," *ArchCl* 25 (1973) 103–122. [p. 116, n. 48 Daedalic hairstyle on frieze plaques]

CAMPOREALE 1972 [1974]

Giovannangelo Camporeale, "Cultura chiusina arcaica," in *Aspetti e problemi dell'Etruria interna: Atti dell'VIII Convegno Nazionale di Studi Etruschi ed Italici, Orvieto 27–30 giugno 1972* (Leo S. Olschki, Florence 1974) 99–130. [p. 110 relation between Poggio Civitate and Chiusi]

CAMPOREALE 1984

Giovannangelo Camporeale, *La Caccia in Etruria* (Giorgio Bretschneider, Rome 1984). [pp. 116, 119, and pl. 45a raking sima, Inv. 68–150]

CAPUTO 1970

Giacomo Caputo, review of *POGGIO CIVITATE* 1970A–B in *StEtr* 38 (1970) 409–411.

CAPUTO 1972 [1974]

Giacomo Caputo, "Cultura orientalizzante dell'Arno," in *Aspetti e problemi dell'Etruria interna: Atti dell'VIII Convegno Nazionale di Studi Etruschi ed Italici, Orvieto 27–30 giugno 1972* (Leo S. Olschki, Florence 1974) 19–66. [p. 51 indirect reference to 'bone lady', Inv. 71–100]

CATENI 1985 (?)

Gabriele Cateni, *The Etruscans* (Regione Lazio/ Assessorato al Turismo, Istituto Geografico Agostino, 1985 [?]). [p. 43]

CHRISTIANSEN 1988

Jette Christiansen, "Some Early Etruscan Revetment Plaques in the Ny Carlsberg Glyptotek," *Acta Hyperborea* 1 (1988) 91–92. [p. 92 frieze plaques from Poggio Civitate]

CIACCI 1981

Andrea Ciacci, "La valle dell'Ombrone," in *Gli Etruschi in Maremma: Popolamento e attività produttive*, ed. Mauro Cristofani (Silvana, Milan 1981) 131–135. [fig. 93 plan; fig. 94 'il cowboy', Inv. 67–411; fig. 95 sphinx, Inv. 68–500]

CIACCI 1985 (?)

Andrea Ciacci, *Etruschi* (Ente Provinciale per il Turismo Siena, Siena 1985 [?]). [pp. 20–21; numerous color ills. passim]

CIMINO 1984

Lea Cimino, "Due novi buccheri a cilindretto di tipo Chiusino," *Prospettiva* 37 (1984) 44–47. [refers to DONATI 1971 and bucchero fragments with horse and rider; connection with horse-race frieze plaques]

CIMINO 1986

Lea Cimino, *La collezione Mieli nel Museo archeologico di Siena* (Giorgio Bretschneider, Rome 1986). [pp. 26, 89, 94]

COARELLI 1983

Filippo Coarelli, *Il Foro Romano* (Quasar, Rome 1983). [p. 61 comparison between the Regia, Poggio Civitate, and Acquarossa]

COLONNA 1973

Giovanni Colonna, "Ricerche sull'Etruria interna Volsiniese," *StEtr* 41 (1973) 45–72, pls. 16–23. [p. 70 Poggio Civitate as meeting place for a minor league]

COLONNA 1980 [1984]

Giovanni Colonna, "I Dauni nel contesto storico e culturale dell'Italia arcaica," in *La civiltà dei Dauni nel quadro del mondo italico: Atti del XIII Convegno di Studi Etruschi e Italici, Manfredonia 21–27 giugno 1980* (Leo S. Olschki, Florence 1984) 263–277, pls. 43–47. [p. 271 seated statues from Poggio Civitate with helmets and pointed hats]

COLONNA 1981

Giovanni Colonna, "Tarquinio Prisco e il Tempio di Giove Capitolino," in *Lazio arcaico e mondo greco: Il convegno di Roma, PP* 36 (1981) 41–59. [p. 46 size of buildings at Poggio Civitate; p. 53, n. 39 square enclosure in courtyard; pp. 57–58 architectural decoration]

COLONNA AND VON HASE 1984 [1986]

Giovanni Colonna and Fr.-W. von Hase, "Alle origini della statuaria etrusca: la tomba delle statue presso Ceri," *StEtr* 52 (1984) [1986] 13–59. [p. 40 seated statues; p. 46 furniture on frieze plaques; pp. 52, 54 akroteria from first and second buildings]

COLONNA 1987

Giovanni Colonna, "Il maestro dell'Ercole e della Minerva. Nuova luce sull'attività dell'officina veiente," *OpRom* 16:1 (1987) 7–41. [p. 24 technique of modeling of statues from Poggio Civitate; n. 60 reference to WINTER 1978]

CRADDOCK 1978

Paul T. Craddock, "Report on the Construction and Composition of the Belt Clasps," StEtr 46 (1978) 54–55 in SWADDLING AND CRADDOCK 1978. [technical analysis of belt clasps in the British Museum]

CRISTOFANI 1972

Mauro Cristofani, "Contributi al più antico bucchero decorato a rilievo, II Osservazioni sul kyathos di Monteriggioni," *StEtr* 40 (1972) 84–94. [p. 87, reference to *StEtr* 39 [1971] 412, Inv. 69–92]

CRISTOFANI 1972 [1974]

Mauro Cristofani, "Intervento," in *Aspetti e problemi dell'Etruria interna: Atti dell'VIII Convegno Nazionale di Studi Etruschi ed Italici, Orvieto, 27–30 giugno 1972* (Leo S. Olschki, Florence 1974) 147–148. [discussion of the ivories published in *AJA* 76 (1972) pls. 51–53]

CRISTOFANI 1975

Mauro Cristofani, "Considerazioni su Poggio Civitate (Murlo, Siena)," *Prospettiva* 1 (1975) 9–17, figs. 1–15. [summary; interpretation of building and purpose of destruction]

CRISTOFANI 1976

Mauro Cristofani, *Città e campagna nell'Etruria settentrionale* (Banca Popolare dell'Etruria, Arezzo 1976). [pp. 85–91, fig. 106 bronze wrestler, Inv. 71–105; fig. 107 'il cowboy', Inv. 67–411; fig. 108 sphinx, Inv. 68–500; fig. 109 banquet frieze; fig. 110 horserace frieze; fig. 111 seated figures frieze; fig. 112 drawing, seated figures frieze; fig. 113 drawing, procession frieze; fig. 114 antefix with human mask; fig. 115 gorgon antefix; fig. 116 vase, Inv. 68–2]

CRISTOFANI 1978A

Mauro Cristofani, *L'arte degli Etruschi: Produzione e Consumo* (Einaudi, Torino 1978). [pp. 64, 66, 120–121, 131–140; fig. 8 plan; fig. 104 seated statue, Inv. 68–200; figs. 106–109 frieze plaques]

CRISTOFANI 1978B

Mauro Cristofani, *Etruschi: Cultura e Società* (Istituto Geografico de Agostini, Novara 1978). [p. 29 procession frieze; pp. 30–31; p. 35 'il cowboy', Inv. 67–411; p. 37 seated figures frieze; p. 101]

CRISTOFANI 1979

Mauro Cristofani, "Recent Advances in Etruscan Epigraphy and Language," in *Italy Before the Romans: The Iron Age, Orientalizing and Etruscan Periods*, ed. David and Francesca S. Ridgway (Academic Press , London and New York, 1979) 373–412. [pp. 381–382 tiles with letters; reference to CRISTOFANI AND PHILLIPS 1971]

CRISTOFANI 1979 [1981]

Mauro Cristofani, "Riflessioni sulla decorazione architettonica di prima fase in Etruria e a Roma," in *Gli Etruschi e Roma. Atti dell'incontro di studio in onore di Massimo Pallottino, Roma, 11–13 dicembre 1979* (Giorgio Bretschneider, Rome 1981) 189–198. [passim]

CRISTOFANI 1985A

Mauro Cristofani, *I bronzi degli Etruschi* (Istituto geografico de Agostini, Novara 1985). [p. 289, no. 110, ref. to PHILLIPS 1984, Inv. 68–196]

CRISTOFANI 1985B

Mauro Cristofani, *Dizionario della civiltà etrusca* (Giunti Martello, Florence 1985). [p. 4 'il cowboy', Inv. 67–411; pp. 181–182 with figs. of plan and of 'il cowboy'; pp. 233–234 with ill. of terracotta stand, Inv. 67–450; p. 264 Chiusine letter forms at Poggio Civitate]

CRISTOFANI 1987

Mauro Cristofani, *Saggi di Storia Etrusca Arcaica* (Giorgio Bretschneider, Rome 1987). [p. 92 interpretation of building; p. 130, n. 63 inscription 'mi avil' from ivory lion head, Inv. 71–500]

CRISTOFANI AND OTHERS 1983

Umberto Baldini, Mauro Cristofani, Guglielmo Maetzke, *Arte in Toscana* (Electa, Milan 1983). [p. 44, fig. 53, banquet frieze, seated figures frieze; fig. 55 sphinx, Inv. 68–500, fig. 56 'il cowboy', Inv. 67–411]

CRISTOFANI AND OTHERS 1984

Mauro Cristofani, Michel Gras, William V. Harris, Adriano Maggiani, Marina Martelli, Helmut Rix, Erika Simon, and Mario Torelli, *Gli Etruschi: una nuova immagine* (Giunti Martello, Florence 1984. [pp. 84, 95, 110–112, 125–126, 178–179, 181; p. 110 plan of building; p. 112 'il cowboy', Inv. 67–411; p. 126 terracotta stand, Inv. 67–450; p. 183 terracotta griffin head, Inv. 68–50]

CRISTOFANI AND OTHERS 1987

Mauro Cristofani, ed., *Etruria e Lazio arcaico. Atti dell'Incontro di Studio (10–11 novembre 1986)* (Quaderni del Centro di Studio per l'Archeologia etrusco-italica, 15; Consiglio Nazionale delle Ricerche, Rome 1987). [p. 63 in Giovanni Colonna, "Etruria e Lazio nell'età dei Tarquini," 55–66; pp. 96–97 in Cristofani, "I santuari: tradizioni decorative," 95–120]

D'AGOSTINO 1983

Bruno d'Agostino, "L'immagine, la pittura e la tomba nell'Etruria arcaica," *BdA* 32 (1983) 2–12. [pp. 5–6 early date of banquet frieze plaques from Poggio Civitate; political power of lord in palace]

DAL MASO AND VENDITTI 1984

Cinzia Dal Maso and Antonio Venditti, *Le Città degli Etruschi* (Bonechi, Florence 1984). [p. 59 text; color ill. of horserace frieze]

DE PALMA 1974

Claudio de Palma, *Testimonianze etrusche* (Il Fiorino, Firenze 1974). [pp. 85, 93, 115, 123, 130, 147–151 description of excavations and surroundings; p. 284 site photographs]

DE PUMA 1986

Richard D. De Puma, *Etruscan Tomb Groups* (von Zabern, Mainz 1986). [pp. 35, 44 date of pottery]

DE RUYT 1987

Franz De Ruyt, review of Warden 1985, in *AntCl* 56 (1987) 542–543.

DENNIS, ED. HEMPHILL 1985

George Dennis, *The Cities and Cemeteries of Etruria*, ed. Pamela Hemphill (Princeton University Press, Princeton 1985). [Introduction, p. xxxiii]

DI MARTINO 1982–1983

Ugo Di Martino, *Gli Etruschi. Storia, civiltà, cultura* (Mursia, Milan 1982–1983). [p. 263 list of sites, # 13 Murlo (Poggio Civitate)]

DI MINO 1982

Maria Rita Di Mino, "Note sulla decorazione coroplastica a Roma dal VI al IV secolo a.C.," in *Roma Repubblicana fra il 509 e il 270 a.C.* (Quasar, Rome 1982) 65–76. [p. 65 use of architectural terracottas at Poggio Civitate and Acquarossa on private and civic structures]

DONATI 1981

Luigi Donati, *La collezione Ciacci nel Museo Archeologico di Grosseto* (De Luca, Rome 1981). [p. 29, p. 33 no. 37, p. 54, no. 92, p. 57, no. 101, p. 62, no. 107]

DONATI 1984

Luigi Donati, *The Antiquities from Saturnia in the University of California Museum at Berkeley*, in *Atti e Memorie dell'accademia toscana di scienze e lettere* XLIV n.s. XXXV (1984) pp. 44 and plates. [p. 13 reference to BOULOUMIÉ 1978, p. 96, no. 371, pl. XX; pp. 13–14 to BOULOUMIÉ 1978, pp. 60 ff., form E1, pl. XXVI, Murlo Inv. 71–212 and 71–185; p. 27 comparison between 8/2202 and BOULOUMIÉ 1978, pp. 94 ff., form M2]

DONATI 1984 [1988]

Luigi Donati, "Roselle (Grosseto). — Le ceramiche di due pozzetti in roccia sulla collina settentrionale," *NSc* 1984, 69–94. [pp. 73, 75, 76, 79, 82]

DONATI 1987

Luigi Donati, "Bucchero, ceramica etrusco-corinzia, ceramica fine a decorazione lineare dipinta, ceramica etrusca a figure rosse," in AA.VV. *Artimino (Firenze), Scavi 1974*, ed. G. Capecchi (Comune di Carmignano, Museo archeologico di Artimino, Florence 1987) 82–103. [pp. 83, 98, 99]

DONATI 1989

Luigi Donati, *Le Tombe da Saturnia nel Museo Archeologico di Firenze* (Leo S. Olschki, Florence 1988). [pp. 68, 126, 128, 135, 136, 145, 148, 162]

DOWNEY 1986

Susan B. Downey, review of RYSTEDT 1983, STRANDBERG OLOFSSON 1984, and Charlotte Scheffer, *Acquarossa II, part 2, The Cooking Stands* (Stockholm 1982), in *AJA* 90 (1986) 491–492.

DREWS 1981

Robert Drews, "The coming of the city to Central Italy," *American Journal of Ancient History* 6 (1981) 133–165. [p. 155 monumental building at Poggio Civitate]

DUMÉZIL 1974

G. Dumézil, *La religion romaine archaïque* (Payot, Paris 1974, 2nd ed.). [p. 669, n. 5 does not accept seated figures frieze as divine triads]

GLI ETRUSCHI 1985

AA. VV., *Gli Etruschi: Mille anni di civiltà*, vol. 2, ed. Giovanni Camporeale and Gabriela Morolli (Bonecchi, Florence 1985). [pp. 475–479; p. 475 ivory gorgon, Inv. 71–102; p. 476 bone handle, Inv. 71–283; p. 479 ivory disk, Inv. 71–118; fanciful reconstruction drawings of building]

FERRI 1978

Silvio Ferri, "Osservazioni ad alcune statue del Murlo-Poggio Civitate (Siena)," *RendLinc* 33 (1978) 3–8, figs. 2–7. [interpretation of seated statues as priests and of monumental building as 'templum'; umbro-celtic connections; fig. 2 'il cowboy', Inv. 67–411; fig. 3 upper torso, Inv. 68–200; figs. 4–5 lower body, Inv. 67–411; fig. 6 helmeted head, Inv. 69–200; figs. 7–7a helmeted head, Inv. 69–277]

FRACCHIA AND GUALTIERI 1989

Helena M. Fracchia and Maurizio Gualtieri, "The Social Context of Cult Practices in pre-Roman Lucania," *AJA* 93 (1989) 217–232. [p. 229, n. 44 references to Murlo and Acquarossa]

FRAZER 1980

Alfred Frazer, "The American contribution to Italian archaeology," in *The Preservation and Use of Artistic Cultural Heritage: Perspectives and Solutions. The Metropolitan Museum of Art, New York 27/28/29 May 1980*, pp. 78–85. [pp. 79–82 summary of site]

FUSAI 1987

Luca Fusai, *La Storia di Siena dalle origini al 1559* (il Leccio, Siena 1987). [p. 13, identification of Poggio Civitate with the Shrine of Voltumna; p. 15]

GEMPELER 1974

Robert D. Gempeler, *Die etruskischen Kanopen: Herstellung, Typologie, Entwicklungsgeschichte* (Einsiedeln 1974). [p. 218 reference to sphinx, Inv. 68–500; p. 225 head, Inv. 68–100]

GRAN AYMERICH 1976

José M.J. Gran Aymerich, "À propos des vases 'à tenons perforés' et du thème des personnages assises," *MélRome* 88:2 (1976) 397–454. [pp. 434–435 reference to BIANCHI BANDINELLI 1972; definition of primitive style; pl. 11, fig. 5 'il cowboy', Inv. 67–411; p. 420 N3 seated statues]

GRANT 1978

Michael Grant, "A View of the Etruscans: Presidential Address Delivered to the Classical Association in the University of Edinburgh, 30 March 1978," *Proceedings of the Classical Association (University of Edinburgh)* 75 (1978) 9–22. [p. 20 cultural sway of Chiusi]

GRANT 1980

Michael Grant, *The Etruscans* (Scribner's, New York 1980). [pp. 213–214; 245; ill. 'il cowboy', Inv. 67–411]

GRAS 1984

Michel Gras, "Canthare, société étrusque et monde grec," *Opus* 3:2 (1984) 325–337. [pp. 329–330]

GRAS 1985

Michel Gras, *Trafics Tyrrhéniens archaïques* (Bibliothèque des écoles françaises d'Athènes et de Rome, 258) Rome 1985 [p. 343 amphoras at Poggio Civitate; pp. 429–430 comparison between Montetosto and Poggio Civitate]

GRECO 1988

Giovanna Greco, "Bilan critique des fouilles de Serra di Vaglio, Lucanie," *RA* 1988:2, 263–290. [p. 278 n. 41 references to friezes at Acquarossa and Poggio Civitate]

HAMBLIN 1975

Dora Jane Hamblin, *The Etruscans* (Time-Life Books, New York 1975). [p. 100 'temple'; pp. 143–146; ill. p. 143 'il cowboy', Inv. 67–411]

HANNESTAD 1982

Lise Hannestad, *Etruskerne og deres kunst* (Sfinx, Aarhus 1982). [pp. 26, 42–43; fig. 44 'il cowboy', Inv. 67–411; fig. 45 seated figures frieze]

HAYES 1985

John W. Hayes, *Etruscan and Italic Pottery in the Royal Ontario Museum* (Royal Ontario Museum, Toronto, Ontario 1985). [pp. 62, 63 bucchero fired red]

HAYNES 1985

Sybille Haynes, *Etruscan Bronzes* (Sotheby's Publications, London and New York 1985). [p. 104 Poggio Civitate as center around Chiusi; cat. 11, pp. 135, 248–249 comparison between British Museum and Poggio Civitate belt clasps]

HESS AND PASCHINGER 1980

Robert Hess and Elfriede Paschinger, *Das etruskische Italien* (DuMont, Köln 1980). [pp. 71–72]

HÖCKMANN 1977

Ursula Höckmann, "Zur Darstellung auf einer 'tyrrhenischen' Amphora in Leipzig," in *Festschrift für Frank Brommer*, ed. U. Höckmann and A. Krug (von Zabern, Mainz 1977) 181–185 [seated figures and procession; divine figures and sacred wedding, Peleus and Thetis]

HUS 1980

Alain Hus, *Les Étrusques et leurs destin* (Picard, Paris 1980). [pp. 81–125 passim; p. 109 plan of building]

JANNOT 1984

Jean-René Jannot, *Les reliefs archaïques de Chiusi* (Collection de l'école française de Rome, vol. 71, Rome 1984). [passim; discussion of seated figures frieze, horserace frieze, raking sima, and terracotta stand, Inv. 67–450]

JANNOT 1986

Jean-René Jannot, "Les cavaliers étrusques," *RM* 96 (1986) 109–133 [p. 125 terracotta stand, Inv. 67–450]

JANNOT 1987

Jean-René Jannot, "Les 'Amazones' de Capoue et les 'jockeys' de Murlo," *Latomus* 46 (1987) 693–703. [pp. 699–703; fig. 11 horserace frieze]

JOHANNOWSKY 1983

Werner Johannowsky, *Materiali di età arcaica dalla Campania* (G. Macchiaroli, Naples 1983). [p. 75, n. 393 Daedalic heads at Poggio Civitate; p. 76, n. 395 lateral sima with feline spout and rosettes compared to sima at Pompeii]

KRAUSKOPF 1988

Ingrid Krauskopf, "Gorgones (in Etruria)," in *LIMC* IV:1–2 (Artemis, Zürich and Munich 1988), 330–345. [no. 1 ivory gorgon, Inv. 71–102; no. gorgon antefix, with ills.]

LATTES 1985

Wanda Lattes, *Gli Etruschi: Guida pratica alle mostre in Toscana* (Florence 1985). [color plate of bronze umpire, Inv. 71–106]

LUNDGREN AND WENDT 1982

Maja-Brita Lundgren and Leni Wendt, *Acquarossa, Vol. III. Zone A*, Stockholm 1982 (*Acta Instituti Romani Regni Sueciae*, series in 4°, 38:III). [pp. 35, 37 reference to BOULOUMIÉ-MARIQUE 1978]

MAASKANT-KLEIBRINK 1987

Marianne Maaskant-Kleibrink, *Settlement Excavations at Borgo Le Ferriere "Satricum"*, vol. 1, *The Campaigns 1979, 1980, 1981* (E. Forsten, Groningen 1987). [esp. pp. 95–105; reference to Poggio Civitate pp. 101, 103 (pl. 47), 105]

MAASKANT-KLEIBRINK 1991

Marianne Maaskant-Kleibrink, "Early Latin Settlement-plans at Borgo Le Ferriere. (*Satricum*)." *BaBesch* 66 (1991) 51–114.

MARTELLI 1978

Marina Martelli, "La ceramica greco-orientale in Etruria," in *Les céramiques de la Grèce de l'est et leur diffusion en occident. Centre Jean Bérard, Institut Français de Naples 6–9 juillet 1976* (Editions du Centre national de la recherche scientifique, Paris 1978). [p. 171 Samian lekythoi; p. 173 reference to *POGGIO CIVITATE* 1970, p. 68, no. 170; p. 198, nos. 127–131 Ionian kylikes, reference to *AJA* 75 (1971) p. 258, pl. 58, figs. 1–3 and 78 (1974) pp. 268–270, figs. 3–6, and pls. 55, figs. 6–7, 56, figs. 4–5; p. 201, nos. 189–194, references to *StEtr* 39 (1971) pp. 415–418; *AJA* 75 (1971), p. 258, pl. 58, fig. 5]

MARTELLI 1979A

Marina Cristofani Martelli, "Un gruppo di placchette eburnee etrusche nei musei di Bologna, Parma, e Rouen," *RA* 1979, 73–86. [p. 35]

MARTELLI 1979B

Marina Cristofani Martelli, "Osservazioni sulle 'stele' di Populonia," in *Studi per Enrico Fiumi* (Pacini, Pisa 1979) 33–45. [p. 84 fig. 18, p. 85, n. 36]

MARTELLI 1979C

Marina Martelli, "Prime Considerazioni sulla statistica delle importazioni greche in Etruria nel periodo arcaico," *StEtr* 47 (1979) 37–52. [p. 52 appendix on Laconian pottery; reference to *AJA*, 81, 1977, 97–98; fig. 31, Inv. 71–769; fig. 32, Inv. 74–30; fig. 33, Inv. 74–30; fig. 34, Inv. 34–31]

MARTELLI 1981

Marina Martelli, "Un sigillo etrusco," *Quaderni Urbinati di Cultura Classica* n.s. 9 (1981) 169–172. [pp. 170, nn. 6,7,8, 171; serpentine seals, Inv. 75–99, 72–160; ivory lion head with inscription, Inv. 71–500]

MASSA-PAIRAULT 1985

Françoise-Hélène Massa-Pairault, *Recherches sur l'art et l'artisanat étrusco-italiques à l'époque hellénistique* (Bibliothèque des écoles françaises d'Athènes et de Rome, 257, Rome 1985). [pp. 6, n. 27; 7, n. 31, 63]

MASSA-PAIRAULT 1986

Françoise-Hélène Massa-Pairault, "Chronique d'archéologie et d'histoire étrusques. Les expositions de "l'année étrusque" en Toscane et en Ombrie," *RA* 1986:2 (1986) 335–369. [pp. 356–357 discussion of Poggio Civitate]

MASSA-PAIRAULT 1988

Françoise-Hélène Massa-Pairault, "La culture en mouvement. *Archéologie.* Les étrusques," in *Encyclopaedia Universalis, "Volume de l'Année"* (Encyclopaedia Universalis, Paris 1988) 399–402. [p. 402]

MAZZESCHI 1976

Enzo Mazzeschi, *Cronache d'Archeologia Senese* (Cantagalli, Siena 1976). [pp. 60–64; reconstruction drawing of courtyard with flanking buildings and ridgepole akroteria, fig. 9]

MELIS 1986

"Considerazioni e ricerche antiquarie su un gruppo di lastre fittili ceretane," in *Italian Iron Age Artefacts in the British Museum. Papers of the Sixth British Museum Colloquium,* ed. Judith Swaddling (British Museum Publications, London 1986), 159–169. [p. 162 frieze plaques from Poggio Civitate]

MENGOZZI 1911

N. Mengozzi, *Il feudo del Vescovado di Siena* (Lazzeri, Siena 1911; repr. Pugliese, Florence 1980). [p. 259 reference to le Civitate]

MERTENS 1980

Dieter Mertens, "Parallelismi strutturali nell'architettura della Magna Grecia e dell'Italia centrale in età arcaica," in *Attività archeologica in Basilicata 1964–1977: Scritti in onore di Dinu Adamesteanu* (Meta, Matera 1980) 37–82. [n. 96 antefixes, ref. to WINTER 1977; n. 97 akroteria, ref. to EDLUND (GANTZ) 1972]

MEYER 1983

J.C. Meyer, *Pre-Republican Rome* (*AnalRom,* Suppl. XI, Odense 1983). [chronology and architectural terracottas, pp. 62, 143, 158–159]

MOSCATI 1973

Sabatino Moscati, *Italia archeologica,* vol. 2 (De Agostini, Novara 1973). [p. 99 description of site, with ill. of lateral sima head]

MOSCATI 1976

Sabatino Moscati, *Le pietre parlano. Alla Scoperta dell'Italia sepolta* (Mondadori, Milan 1976). [pp. 89–95 summary; fig. 21 banquet frieze; fig. 22 sphinx, Inv. 68–500]

MOSCATI 1984

Sabatino Moscati, *Italia Ricomparsa: Etrusca Italica* (Touring Club Italiano, Milan 1984). [pp. 40–47, figs. 25–42: fig. 25 ivory animal, Inv. 71–282; fig. 26, ivory griffin, Inv. 71–101; fig. 27, ivory gorgon, Inv. 71–102; fig. 28, bone disk, Inv. 71–103; fig. 29, bone disk, Inv. 71–118; fig. 30, bronze umpire, Inv. 71–106; fig. 31 ivory ram, Inv. 71–92; fig. 32 ivory sphinx, Inv. 71–198; fig. 33 bronze wrestler, Inv. 71–105; fig. 34 procession frieze fragment; fig. 35 feline protome, fig. 36 gorgon antefix; fig. 37 horserace frieze; fig. 38, horserace frieze; fig. 39 horserace frieze; fig. 40 horserace frieze detail; fig. 41 'il cowboy', Inv. 67–411; fig. 42 sphinx, Inv. 68–500]

MÜHLESTEIN 1929

H. Mühlestein, *Die Kunst der Etrusker* (Frankfurter Verlags-Anstalt, Berlin 1929). [pp. 225–226 description of belt buckle from Poggio Civitate, illustrated on fig. 142]

MURRAY 1985

Oswyn Murray, "At the Etruscan banquet," *Times Literary Supplement*, August 30, 1985, pp. 948 and 960. [review article of exhibition catalogues including AREZZO *SE*, 1985; FLORENCE *CE*, 1985; SIENA *CP*, 1985, and VOLTERRA AND CHIUSI 1985]

ORLANDINI 1978

Piero Orlandini, "L'Arte dell'Italia preromana," in *Popoli e Civiltà dell'Italia antica* Vol. 7 (Biblioteca di Storia Patria, Rome 1978) 239–286, pls. 72. [pp. 248–249 Poggio Civitate and Acquarossa; pl. 28b 'il cowboy', Inv. 67–411; pl. 29a horserace frieze]

ORLANDINI 1983

Piero Orlandini, in *Megale Hellas. Storia e civiltà della Magna Grecia* ('Antica madre' Credito Italiano, Milan 1983). [p. 355 frieze plaques]

PALLOTTINO 1971

Massimo Pallottino, *Civiltà artistica etrusco-italica* (Sansoni, Florence 1971). [pp. 76, 78, 83]

PALLOTTINO 1975

Massimo Pallottino, *The Etruscans: Revised and Enlarged.* Translated by J. Cremona. Ed. David Ridgway (Indiana University Press, Bloomington and London 1975). [pp. 121, 235, 238, 258]

PALLOTTINO 1984

Massimo Pallottino, *Etruscologia*, 7th ed. (Hoepli, Milan 1984). [pp. 15, 32, 131, 133, 183, 264, 291, 297, 400; fig. 11 below, plan of building; pl. xcii 'il cowboy', Inv. 67–411]

PASSERI 1985

Vincenzo Passeri, *I Castelli del Comune di Murlo* (Studium editrice, Radda in Chianti 1985). [p. 57 reference to the location of 'Civitate']

PELLEGRINI 1902

G. Pellegrini, "Appendice Museografica — Siena, Museo Chigi, I Bronzi," in *Studi e Materiali di Archeologia e Numismatica* 2 (1902) 207–222. [p. 211 bronze belt buckle; cf. MÜHLESTEIN 1929]

PENSABENE AND DI MINO 1983

Ministero per i beni culturali e ambientali: Soprintendenza archeologica di Roma. Patrizio Pensabene e Maria Rita Sanzi Di Mino, *Museo Nazionale Romano: Le Terrecotte III.1: Antefisse* (De Luca, Rome 1983). [p. 25, n. 10 archaic antefixes from Minturnae, Capua, and Poggio Civitate]

PFIFFIG 1975

A.J. Pfiffig, *Religio etrusca* (Akademische Druck-und Verlagsanstalt, Graz 1975). [p. 36 and fig. 2 does not accept seated figures frieze as divine triads]

PIANU 1985

Giampiero Pianu, *Gli Etruschi. Cinque miti da sfatare* (Armando Curcio, Rome 1985). [pp. 134–140 comparison between monumental buildings ('palazzi') at Acquarossa and Poggio Civitate, with plans on pages 136 (Acquarossa) and 139 (Poggio Civitate)]

PIGGOT 1983

S. Piggot, *The Earliest Wheeled Transport* (Thames & Hudson, London 1983). [p. 181 cart on procession frieze]

PRAYON 1975

Friedhelm Prayon, *Frühetruskische Grab-und Hausarchitektur* (*RM-EH* 22, Heidelberg 1975). [pp. 133–135 description of monumental building; pp. 146, 147, 157, 162, 166, 179, 181; Pl. 88.11]

PUGLIESE CARRATELLI 1986

Giovanni Pugliese Carratelli, ed., *Rasenna Storia e Civiltà degli Etruschi* ('Antica madre', Credito Italiano, Milan 1986). [no index; duplication of plans and objects, but not identical; pp. 47, 261–262, 283, 372, 424–426, 434, 443, 445, 461, 470, 492, 703–704; fig. 160 seated figures frieze; Tav. III plan of building; figs. 296–298 'il cowboy', Inv. 67–411, seated figures frieze, banquet frieze; Tav. XIV plan of building; fig. 466 horseman akroterion; figs. 507 procession frieze; fig. 521 terracotta stand, Inv. 67–450; fig. 522 'il cowboy', upper body; figs. 522–527 sphinx, Inv. 68–500; terracotta head, Inv. 68–100]

REICH 1979

John Reich, *Italy Before Rome* (Elsevier-Phaidon, Oxford 1979). [pp. 7, 8, 90 description of site]

RICHARDSON 1976

Emeline Richardson, *The Etruscans. Their Art and Civilization* (University of Chicago Press, Chicago and London, 1976). [pp. 250–251]

RICHARDSON 1983

Emeline Richardson, *Etruscan Votive Bronzes, Geometric, Orientalizing, Archaic* (von Zabern, Mainz am Rhein 1983). [pp. 33 and 93 pointed shoes on seated statues; pp. 73 and 154 curved staff on seated figures frieze; p. 90 architectural terracottas; p. 338 seated statues]

RIDGWAY 1981

David Ridgway, *The Etruscans* (The University of Edinburgh, Department of Archaeology: Occasional Paper no. 6, 1981). [p. 11; pp. 27–28; local preprint for Ridgway 1988]

RIDGWAY 1983

David Ridgway, review of SCHEFFER 1981, LUNDGREN AND WENDT 1982, and Charlotte Wikander, *Acquarossa I, part 1, The Painted Architectural Terracottas* (Stockholm 1981), in *CR* 33 (1983) 365–366

RIDGWAY 1987

David Ridgway, review of RYSTEDT 1983, STRANDBERG OLOFSSON 1984, and Charlotte Scheffer, *Acquarossa II, part 2, The Cooking Stands* (Stockholm 1982), in *CR* 37:1 (1987) 74–76.

RIDGWAY 1988

David Ridgway, "The Etruscans," ch. 13 in *The Cambridge Ancient History*, vol. IV (Cambridge University Press, Cambridge 1988, 634–675. [p. 640; p. 666; p. 668; ills. in plate volume: pl. 292a horserace frieze; pl. 292b banquet frieze; pl. 292c 'il cowboy', Inv. 67–411]

RIDGWAY AND RIDGWAY 1984

Francesca R. Serra Ridgway and David Ridgway, review of RYSTEDT 1983, in *StEtr* 52 (1984) 544–554.

RIEDEL 1982

Alfred Riedel, "The Paleovenetian Horse of Le Brustolade," *StEtr* 50 (1982) 227–256. [p. 235 reference to AZZAROLI 1972 and horse from Poggio Civitate]

RIIS 1981

P.J. Riis, *Etruscan Types of Heads: A Revised Chronology of the Archaic and Classical Terracottas of Etruscan Campania and Central Italy* (Det Kongelige Danske Videnskabernes Selskab, Historisk-filosofiske Skrifter 9:5, Copenhagen 1981). [pp. 68–74 discussion of style and chronology; affinities with Chiusi]

RINARD 1979

Judith E. Rinard, "Etruscans: Festive in Life, Lavish in Death," in *Mysteries of the Ancient World* (National Geographic Society, Washington 1979). [p. 186 color ill. of 'il cowboy', Inv. 67–411]

SALSKOV ROBERTS 1988

Helle Salskov Roberts, "Some Observations on Etruscan Bowls with Supports in the Shape of Caryatids or Adorned by Reliefs," *Acta Hyperborea* 1 (1988) 69–80. [pp. 78–79 and fig. 6b frieze plaques from Poggio Civitate]

SOMMELLA MURA 1981

Anna Sommella Mura, "Il gruppo di Ercole e Athena," in *Lazio arcaico el mondo greco; Il convegno di Roma, PP* 36 (1981) 59–64. [p. 64, nn. 6, 8 interpretation of frieze plaques from Poggio Civitate]

SPRENGER AND BARTOLONI 1977

Maja Sprenger and Gilda Bartoloni, *Die Etrusker: Kunst und Geschichte* (Hirmer, Munich 1977). [fig. 54 sphinx, Inv. 68–500; fig. 55 'il cowboy', Inv. 67–411; fig. 56, head Inv. 68–100; fig. 57 horserace, banquet, and seated figures friezes; Abb. 16 plan]

STACCIOLI 1976

Romolo A. Staccioli, "Considerazioni sui complessi monumentali di Murlo e di Acquarossa," in *Mélanges offerts à Jacques Heurgon: L'Italie préromaine et la Rome républicaine, Collection de l'école française de Rome*, vol. 27, part 2 (1976) 961–972. [interpretation of building; question of symmetry and monumentality; fig. 1 plan]

STACCIOLI 1985

Romolo A. Staccioli, *Guide officiel du "Progetto Etruschi"* [published in several languages] (Electa, Milan 1985). [pp. 90–93 text; fig. 47 seated figures frieze drawing; fig. 48 procession frieze drawing; fig. 49 plan of building; fig. 50 'il cowboy', Inv. 67–411]

STAMBAUGH 1988

John E. Stambaugh, *The Ancient Roman City* (The Johns Hopkins University Press, Baltimore 1988). [p. 215 reference to interpretation of the small enclosure in the courtyard of the Archaic Building as a 'templum', PHILLIPS 1972]

STARY 1981

P.F. Stary, *Zur eisenzeitlichen Bewaffnung und Kampfesweise in Mittelitalien (ca. 9. bis 6. Jh. v. Chr.)* (*Marburg Studien zur Vor- und Frühgeschichte* 3, von Zabern, Mainz am Rhein 1981). [pl. 21, no. 3 terracotta stand, Inv. 67–450; pl. 21, no. 4 bucchero rim, Inv. 70–1; mistakenly identifies Inv. 67–450 as bucchero vase]

STEINGRÄBER 1979

Stephan Steingräber, *Etruskische Möbel* (Giorgio Bretschneider, Rome 1979). [p. 226, nos. 131–133; pp. 298–299, no. 527; passim in text]

STEINGRÄBER 1981A

Stephan Steingräber, *Etrurien: Städte, Heiligtümer, Nekropolen* (Hirmer, Munich 1981). [pp. 87–91; fig. 30 plan; fig. 31 'il cowboy', Inv. 67–411]

STEINGRÄBER 1981B

Stephan Steingräber, "Frühe griechische Möbelformen in Etrurien," in *Die Aufnamhme fremder Kultureinflusse in Etrurien und das Problem des Retardierens in der etruskischen Kunst: Schriften des deutschen Archäologen-Verbundes V* (Mannheim 1981) 133–136. [p. 135 furniture on frieze plaques from Poggio Civitate]

STOPPONI 1983

Simonetta Stopponi, *La Tomba della "Scrofa Nera": Materiali del Museo Nazionale di Tarquinia VIII* (Giorgio Bretschneider, Rome 1983). [p. 45 and n. 80 seated figures frieze]

STRANDBERG OLOFSSON 1984

Margareta Strandberg Olofsson, *Acquarossa V:1. The head antefixes and relief plaques. Part 1. A reconstruction of a terracotta decoration and its architectural setting*, Stockholm 1984 (*Acta Instituti Romani Regni Sueciae*, series in 4°, 38:V,1). [pp. 81–82 comparison between Zone F at Acquarossa and the 'square complex' at Poggio Civitate]

STRØM 1986

Ingrid Strøm, "Decorated bronze sheets from a chair," in *Italian Iron Age Artefacts in the British Museum*, Papers of the Sixth British Museum Classical Colloquium, ed. Judith Swaddling (British Museum Publications, London 1986) 53–57. [p. 55, n. 4 throne of Hera on seated figures frieze]

SWADDLING AND CRADDOCK 1978

Judith Swaddling and Paul T. Craddock, "Etruscan Bronze Belt Clasps with Iron Inlay," *StEtr* 46 (1978) 47–55. [pp. 49–50, 51, 52 Murlo belt clasps]

SZILÁGYI 1984

Janos G. Szilágyi, "Tibicen Tuscus," in *Studi di antichità in onore di Guglielmo Maetzke* (Giorgio Bretschneider, Rome 1984). [p. 477, n. 24 reference to SMALL 1971]

THUILLIER 1980

Jean-Paul Thuillier, "À propos des 'Triades Divines' de Poggio Civitate (Murlo)," in *Centre de recherches d'histoire et de philologie de la IVe Section de l'école pratique des hautes études, III Hautes études du monde gréco-romain, vol. 10, Recherches sur les religions de l'antiquité classique* (Droz, Geneva and Paris 1980), by Raymond Bloch and others, 385–394. [fig. 1 seated figures frieze; interpretation of seated figures frieze and horserace frieze as representing an athletic event]

THUILLIER 1981

Jean-Paul Thuillier, "Les sports dans la civilization étrusque," *Stadion: Internazionale Zeitschrift für Geschichte des Sports und der Körperkultur/Journal of the History of Sport and Physical Education* 7:2 (1981) 173–202. [representations from Poggio Civitate of bronze wrestlers and umpire, horserace frieze plaque important for history of Etruscan sports because of early date of site]

THUILLIER 1985

Jean-Paul Thuillier, *Les jeux athlétiques dans la civilisation étrusque* (Bibliothèque des écoles françaises d'Athènes et de Rome, 256, Rome 1985). [pp. 70–77 and figs. 9–10 discussion of bronze group of wrestlers and umpire; pp. 82–87 and fig. 11 horse race; pp. 427–436 function of building and plan, fig. 51; pp. 449–457 and fig. 53 interpretation of seated figures frieze; passim]

TORELLI 1980

Mario Torelli, *Guide archeologiche Laterza: Etruria* (Laterza, Rome and Bari 1980). [pp. 248; 265–268]

TORELLI 1980 [1983]

Mario Torelli, "*Polis* et 'palazzo'. Architettura, ideologia e artigianato greco in Etruria tra VII e VI sec. a.C.," in *Architecture et société de l'archaïsme grec à la fin de la république romaine* (Collection de l'école française de Rome, vol. 66, Rome 1980 [1983]) 471–492. [pp. 478–482; 485–486; 488–489; 492; fig. 6 plan; fig. 7 seated figures frieze]

TORELLI 1981

Mario Torelli, *Storia degli Etruschi* (Laterza, Rome and Bari 1981). [pp. 83–87; 98, 125, 173–175; 180; 186–188; fig. 20 plan, fig. 22 frieze plaques]

TORELLI 1984

Mario Torelli, *Lavinio e Roma* (Quasar, Rome 1984). [p. 148 terracotta plaques; parallels with Metaponto]

TORELLI 1985

Mario Torelli, *L'Arte degli Etruschi*, (Laterza, Rome and Bari 1985). [passim; fig. 10 banquet frieze; fig. 41 head, Inv. 68–100]

TORELLI 1986

Mario Torelli, review of
*Acta Instituti Romani Regni
Sueciae*, series in 4°, *Acquarossa*
38:I,1 (CH. WIKANDER 1981), II
(SCHEFFER 1981), IV (RYSTEDT
1983), V,1 STRANDBERG
OLOFSSON 1984) in *Gnomon*
58 (1986) 259–267.

TORELLI 1987

Mario Torelli, *La società etrusca*
(La Nuova Italia Scientifica,
Rome 1987). [pp. 25, 67–68]

VELLUCCI 1985

Karen Brown Vellucci,
"Etruscan Athletics: Glimpses
of a Clusine Civilization,"
Expedition 27:2 (1985) 22–29.
[pp. 28–29 cauldron on
horserace frieze as prize; cf.
Tomb of the Augurs; fig. 11
Inv. 68–86]

VON HASE 1971

F.-W. Hase, "Gürtelschliessen
des 7. und 6. Jahrhunderts v.
Chr. in Mittelitalien," *JdI* 1971,
1–59. [p. 49, figs. 20–21
bronze clasps from Poggio
Civitate]

VON VACANO 1973

Otto Wilhelm von Vacano,
"Vulca, Rom und die Wölfin:
Untersuchungen zur Kunst
des frühen Rom," in *Aufstieg
und Niedergang der römischen
Welt: Geschichte und Kultur Roms
im Spiegel der neueren Forschung.*
I. *Von den Anfängen Roms bis
zum Ausgang der Republik*, vol.
IV (De Gruyter, Berlin 1973),
ed. Hildegard Temporini,
523–583. [pp. 535–541
description of site; referred to
as 'Heiligtum'; seated figures
frize; seated statues
interpreted as 'Götterbilder']

CH. WIKANDER 1976

Charlotte Wikander, "Painted
Architectural Terracottas from
Acquarossa. A Preliminary
Report," *OpRom* 11:5 (1976)
53–61. [pp. 53, 61]

CH. WIKANDER 1986

Charlotte Wikander, *Sicilian
Architectural Terracottas*,
Stockholm 1986 (*Acta Instituti
Romani Regni Sueciae*, series in
8°, 15). [pp. 11–12]

CH. WIKANDER 1988

Charlotte Wikander,
*Acquarossa Vol. I. The Painted
Architectural Terracottas. Part 2:
Typological and Decorative
Analysis*, Stockholm 1988 (*Acta
Instituti Romani Regni Sueciae*,
series in 4°, 38:I,2). [passim;
pp. 126–130 comparison
between Acquarossa and
Poggio Civitate]

WILLIAMS 1978

Charles K. Williams, II,
"Demaratus and Early
Corinthian Roofs," in
*ΣΤΗΛΗ. ΤΟΜΟΣ ΕΙΣ
ΜΝΗΜΗΝ ΝΙΚΟΛΑΟΥ
ΚΟΝΤΟΛΕΟΝΤΟΣ* (Athens
1978) 345–350. [pp. 349–350
"Murlo now provides the earli-
est date for the use of roof
tiles."]

ZIFFERERO 1980

Andrea Zifferero, *L'abitato
etrusco di piana di Stigliano*
(Gruppo archeologico
romano, Rome 1980).
[passim]

III. Exhibition Catalogues

ALIMENTAZIONE 1987

L'alimentazione nel mondo antico. Gli etruschi, ed. G. Barbieri (Istituto poligrafico e zecca dello stato. Libreria dello stato, Rome 1987). [Scheffer 1987, pp. 97–105; Mauro Cristofani, "Il banchetto in Etruria," pp. 123–132, ref. to banquet frieze from Poggio Civitate p. 126 (with illustration); Carlotta Cianferoni, p. 159 entry no. 36 by Carlotta Cianferoni, terracotta covers, previously discussed in SIENA *CP*, 1985, nos. 653, 654, 655, 656]

AREZZO 1984

Ministero dei Beni Culturali e Ambientali-Soprintendenza Archeologica della Toscana, *Cento preziosi etruschi: Catalogo della mostra dal 7 settembre 1984; centro affari e promozioni; dal 20 ottobre 1984: anfiteatro romano arezzo* ("Il Torchio," Florence 1984). [pp. 126–137: catalogue of ivories, bone objects, precious metals and gems from Poggio Civitate; Erik O. Nielsen, nos. 75–86; Richard

D. De Puma, nos. 87–91; K.M. Phillips, Jr., nos. 92–93; concordance of catalogue numbers and inventory numbers: no. 75: Inv. 71–198; no. 76: Inv. 71–280; no. 77: Inv. 71–92; no. 78: Inv. 71–681; no. 79: Inv. 71–205; no. 80: Inv. 71–283; no. 81: Inv. 71–100; no. 82: Inv. 71–102; no. 83: Inv. 71–101; no. 84: Inv. 71–103; no. 85: Inv. 71–118; no. 86: Inv. 71–282; no. 87: Inv. 71–721, 71–722, 71–723, 71–724, 71–400; no. 88: Inv. 71–721; no. 89: Inv. 72–2; no. 90: Inv. 71–618; no. 91: Inv. 71–669; no. 92: Inv. 75–99; no. 93: Inv. 72–160] [see also *SCHÄTZE DER ETRUSKER* 1986]

AREZZO *SE*, 1985

Regione Toscana, *Santuari d'Etruria,* ed. Giovanni Colonna (Electa, Milan 1985). [Giovanni Colonna, p. 53 section 2.0; Giuliana Nardi, p. 154, entry 8.2.1, reference to sphinx, Inv. 68–500] [reviews by MURRAY 1985; MASSA-PAIRAULT 1986]

BERLIN 1988

Die Welt der Etrusker. Archäologische Denkmäler aus Museen der sozialistischen Länder. Staatliche Museen zu Berlin, Hauptstadt der DDR, Altes Museum, vom 4. Oktober bis 30. Dezember 1988 (Henschelverlag, Berlin 1988). [pp. 25, 154; references in entries B 6.1.1, 6.1.4, and 6.1.8]

ENEA NEL LAZIO 1981

Enea nel Lazio; archeologia e mito. Bimillenario Virgiliano. Roma 22 settembre–31 dicembre 1981. Campidoglio-Palazzo dei Conservatori (Fratelli Palombi Editori, Rome 1981). [Laura Ferrea, p. 131 alabastron, Inv. 66–279; Emilia Talamo, p. 132 gem stone, Inv. 75–99; p. 134 ivory lion, Inv. 71–500]

ETRURIA MINERARIA 1985

Regione Toscana, *L'Etruria mineraria*, ed. Giovannangelo Camporeale (Electa, Milan 1985). [section on Massa Marittima (Lago dell'Accesa), pp. 127–178 has references to BOULOUMIÉ 1978 and BOULOUMIÉ-MARIQUE 1978 passim; bibliography includes BIANCHI BANDINELLI 1972 and MACINTOSH 1974] [reviews by MURRAY 1985; MASSA-PAIRAULT 1986]

FLORENCE *CE*, 1985

Regione Toscana, *Civiltà degli Etruschi*, ed. Mauro Cristofani (Electa, Milan 1985) [Guido Mansuelli, p. 112 section 4 Poggio Civitate as 'unicum'; Antonella Romualdi, p. 152 section 6.23.4 bronze fan; frieze plaques; Piera Melli, p. 158 section 6.31 inscribed tiles; Marina Martelli, p. 232 section 8.9 ivory lion with inscription, Inv. 71–500; Francesca Melis, p. 245 section 9.4 seated figures frieze; p. 265 section 10.9 frieze plaque from Velletri] [reviews by MURRAY 1985; MASSA-PAIRAULT 1986]

MALMÖ, *ETRUSKERNA* 1987

Charlotte and Örjan Wikander, *Etruskerna. Malmö Museum 28.9– 15.11.1987* (Malmö Museers Årsbok 1986–87, Malmö 1987). [pp. 13, 63, 73, and 96 references to Poggio Civitate; fig. 17 plan of building]

MURLO 1988

Comune di Murlo, *Antiquarium di Poggio Civitate* (le tre arti, Florence 1988). Introduction by Romualdo Fracassi (Sindaco di Murlo). [description of site and of objects on display in the Antiquarium at Murlo, opened in July 1988]

POGGIO CIVITATE 1970A

Soprintendenza alle Antichità d'Etruria, *Poggio Civitate (Murlo, Siena): The Archaic Etruscan Sanctuary, Catalogue of the Exhibition, Florence-Siena, 1970* (Leo S. Olschki, Florence 1970). Text by Kyle Meredith Phillips, Jr. and Anna Talocchini. Translations by Luigi Donati and Lisa Mibach. Pp. 80, pls. 44.

POGGIO CIVITATE 1970B

Soprintendenza alle Antichità d'Etruria, *Poggio Civitate (Murlo, Siena): Il Santuario arcaico, Catalogo della Mostra, Firenze-Siena, 1970* (Leo S. Olschki, Firenze 1970). Catalogo a cura del Kyle Meredith Phillips, Jr. e della dott. Anna Talocchini. Traduzione a cura del dott. Luigi Donati e Lisa Mibach.

PRIMA ITALIA 1980 [1981]

Prima Italia: Arts italiques du premier millenaire avant J.C. 5 novembre 1980–4 janvier 1981. Musées Royaux d'Art et d'Histoire, Bruxelles (Musées Royaux d'art et d'histoire, Bruxelles 1980). [Elisabetta Mangani, pp. 135–138, no. 74, banquet frieze, and no. 75 horserace frieze]

PRIMA ITALIA 1981

Prima Italia: L'arte italica del I millennio a.C. Museo Luigi Pigorini, Roma, Piazzale Marconi n. 14–EUR 18 Marzo–30 Aprile 1981 (De Luca, Rome 1981). [Elisabetta Mangani, pp. 120–122, nos. 73, banquet frieze, and 74, horse-race frieze]

ROSELLE 1975

Soprintendenza archeologica della Toscana, *Roselle: Gli scavi e la mostra* (Pacini, Pisa 1975). [p. 38, n. 133 panther protome, Inv. 66–227; n. 134 bucchero stand, Inv. 68–2]

SATRICUM 1982

Comune di Latina, *Satricum: una città latina* (Alinari, Florence 1982). [p. 41; p. 59, n. 7 architectural terracottas at Poggio Civitate and Acquarossa]

SCHÄTZE DER ETRUSKER 1986

Schätze der Etrusker. Ausstellungskatalog (Saarbrücken 1986). [German edition of AREZZO 1984. Pp. 243–251, nos. 1–19; ills. pp. 95–102. Concordance of catalogue numbers and SIENA *CP,* 1985: no. 1: section 3, no. 200; no. 2: 3.201; no. 3: 3.199; no. 4: 3.194; no. 5: 3.195; no. 6: 3.213; no. 7: 3.214; no. 8: 3.209; no. 9: 3.210; no. 10: 3.211; no. 11: 3.212; no. 12: 3.215; no. 13: 3.190a–f; no. 14: 3.188; no. 15: 3.189; no. 16: 3.186; no. 17: 3.187; no. 18: 3.192; no. 19: 3.191]

SIENA 1979

Siena: Le origini. Testimonianze e miti archeologici. Catalogo della Mostra. Siena, Dicembre 1979–Marzo 1980, ed. Mauro Cristofani (Leo S. Olschki, Florence 1979). [pp. 19–24; fig. VI seated statue, Inv. 68–200; fig. VII gorgon antefix; fig. VIII terracotta stand, Inv. 67–450]

SIENA 1986

Elisabetta Mangani and S. Goggioli, *I centri archeologici della provincia di Siena* (Amministrazione Provinciale di Siena, Siena 1986). [pp. 75–81, figs. 3.1–3.6 plans of building, 'il cowboy', Inv. 67–411, raking sima, lateral sima, horserace frieze]

SIENA *CP,* 1985

Regione Toscana, *Case e palazzi d'Etruria*, ed. S. Stopponi (Electa, Milan, 1985). [Section 3 Poggio Civitate (Murlo), pp. 64–69 introduction by Erik O. Nielsen and Kyle M. Phillips; p. 69, nos. 1–6 tiles by Örjan Wikander; pp. 70–73, nos. 7–20 akroteria by Eva Rystedt and Lamar R. Lacy; pp. 73–74, nos. 21–29 raking and lateral simas by Nielsen, Phillips, and Lacy; pp. 74–78, nos. 30–53 Greek pottery by Phillips and Lacy; pp. 78–80, nos. 54–59 Etrusco-Corinthian pottery by Elisabetta Mangani; pp. 80–88, nos. 60–133 Late Orientalizing pottery by Nielsen, Phillips, and Gloria Rosati; pp. 88–92, nos. 134–185 bronzes and iron objects, by P. Gregory Warden, and Lacy; p. 93 nos. 186–193 precious metals and semiprecious stones by Richard D. De Puma, and Lacy; pp. 94–98, nos. 194–215 bone, horn and ivory objects by Nielsen and Lacy; pp. 98–99 text by Nielsen and Phillips; pp. 99–100, nos. 216–241 tiles by Wikander and Lacy; pp. 100–102, nos. 242–257 inscribed tiles by Adriano Maggiani and Lacy; pp. 102–110, nos. 258–303 seated and standing akroteria by Ingrid E.M. Edlund and Lacy; pp. 110–114, nos. 304–326 animal akroteria by Lacy; pp. 114–116, nos. 327–337 gorgons by Lacy; pp. 116–118, nos. 338–342 by Françoise-Hélène Pairault-Massa and Lacy; pp. 118–121, nos. 343–378 lateral sima by Phillips and Lacy; pp. 121–122, nos. 379–384 leopard protomes by Phillips and Lacy; pp. 122–127, nos. 385–436 frieze plaques by Annette Rathje and Lacy; p. 127, nos. 437–438 by Lacy; p. 127 text by Phillips; pp. 127–131, nos.

439–485 bronzes and iron objects by Warden and Lacy; pp. 131–137, nos. 486–532 bucchero by Luigi Donati and Pamela Gambogi; pp. 138–146, nos. 533–643 coarse pottery by Bernard Bouloumié and Lacy; pp. 146–148, nos. 646–659 kitchen ware by Bouloumié and Lacy; pp. 148–149, nos. 660–669 inscribed pottery by Maggiani and Lacy; pp. 149–150, nos. 670–684 terracotta objects by Phillips; pp. 150–154, nos. 685–696 various objects by Phillips; p. 183 Satricum by Marianne Maaskant-Kleibrink and Elisabeth van 't Lindenhout; p. 190 no. 7.9 shod terracotta foot from the Regia by Susan B. Downey] [reviews by MURRAY 1985; MASSA-PAIRAULT 1986]

STOCKHOLM 1972

Associazione Tuscia—Viterbo, *Gli Etruschi: Nuove ricerche e scoperte*. Mostra organizzata nel Museo Storico di Stato a Stoccolma dai seguenti Enti: L'Istituto Svedese di Studi Classici di Roma, Il Museo Mediterraneo di Stoccolma, Il Museo Storico di Stato di Stoccolma, La Soprintendenza alle Antichità dell'Etruria Meridionale. 6 novembre 1972–28 gennaio 1973 (Associazione Tuscia, Viterbo 1972). Pp. 118, disegni e piante 6, tavole 31. [Kyle M. Phillips, Jr., pp. 101–108, no. 193, banquet frieze, Inv. 69–220; no. 194, horserace frieze, Inv. 67–95; no. 195, seated figures frieze, Inv. 68–269; no. 196, procession frieze, Inv. 66–231; no. 197, procession frieze, Inv. 68–393; no. 198, procession frieze, Inv. 66–118; no. 199, procession frieze, Inv. 68–389; no. 200, raking sima, Inv. 68–379, pls. 29–30]

VITERBO 1986

Regione Lazio, *Architettura etrusca nel Viterbese; Ricerche svedesi a San Giovenale e Acquarossa 1956–1986* (De Luca, Rome 1986). [references in the contributions by Anna Maria Sgubini Moretti, Margareta Strandberg Olofsson, Eva Rystedt, Charlotte Wikander, and Örjan Wikander: pp. 60, 65, 78 n. 21, 78 n. 25, 104, 107 n. 4, 108 n. 46, 108 n. 60, 108 n. 63, 108 n. 70, 108 n. 75, 131–132, 134 n. 13, 134, n. 21, 143 n. 24, 143 n. 44]

VOLTERRA AND CHIUSI 1985

Regione Toscana, *Artigianato artistico in Etruria*, ed. Adriano Maggiani (Electa, Milan 1985). [Anna Maria Esposito, p. 138 architectural terracottas, n. 1 ref. to PHILLIPS 1983] [reviews by MURRAY 1985; MASSA-PAIRAULT 1986]

IV. Work in Press and in Preparation

De Puma and Small, eds., in press

Richard D. De Puma and J. Penny Small, eds., *Etruscan Art and Society. Studies on Murlo and Ancient Etruria* (University of Wisconsin Press, Madison, Wisconsin). [a collection of articles on recent Etruscan scholarship. Contributions by Kyle M. Phillips, and by his colleagues and students]

Edlund-Berry, in press

Ingrid E.M. Edlund-Berry, "The Murlo Cowboy: Problems of Reconstruction and Interpretation," in *OpRom*.

Edlund-Berry, in press

Ingrid E.M. Edlund-Berry, "Ritual Destruction of Cities and Sanctuaries: The "Un-founding" of the Archaic Monumental Building at Poggio Civitate," contribution to De Puma and Small, Eds.

Hague Sinos, in press

Rebecca Hague Sinos, "God-like Men: A Discussion of the Murlo Procession Frieze," contribution to De Puma and Small, Eds.

Maggiani, in preparation

Adriano Maggiani, "Inscriptions from Poggio Civitate (Murlo)."

Massa-Pairault, manuscript

Françoise-Hélène Massa-Pairault, "La sima oblique de Murlo. Étude technique, iconographique, stylistique."

Nielsen, in press

Erik O. Nielsen, "Interpreting the Lateral Sima at Poggio Civitate," contribution to De Puma and Small, Eds.

Phillips, in press

Kyle Meredith Phillips, Jr., "Stamped Impasto Pottery Manufactured at Poggio Civitate," contribution to De Puma and Small, Eds.

Phillips and Nielsen, manuscript

Kyle Meredith Phillips, Jr. and Erik O. Nielsen, "Poggio Civitate (Murlo, Siena)," entry in *EAA*, supplement.

Rathje, in press

Annette Rathje, "Banquet and Ideology: Some New Considerations about Banqueting at Poggio Civitate (Murlo)," contribution to De Puma and Small, Eds.

Rathje and von Mehren, in preparation

Annette Rathje and Margit von Mehren, "I: The Ideological Program of the Murlo Frieze" and "II: The Murlo Frieze and its Technical Aspects."

Rowland, in press

Ingrid D. Rowland, "Early Attestations of the Name Poggio Civitate," contribution to De Puma and Small, Eds.

Rowland, in press

Ingrid D. Rowland, "L'*Historia Porsennae* e la conoscenza degli Etruschi nel Rinascimento," in *Studi Umanistici Piceni/Res Publica Litterarum* 9 (1989) 185–193.

Rystedt, in press

Eva Rystedt, "Additional Notes on Early Etruscan Akroteria," contribution to De Puma and Small, Eds.

SMALL, IN PRESS

Jocelyn Penny Small, "Eat, Drink, and Be Merry: Etruscan Banquets," contribution to DE PUMA AND SMALL, EDS.

WIKANDER, IN PREPARATION

Örjan Wikander, "Architectural Terracottas from Poggio Civitate (Murlo)."

WIKANDER, IN PRESS

Örjan Wikander, "The Archaic Etruscan Sima," contribution to DE PUMA AND SMALL, EDS.

WINTER, IN PRESS

Nancy A. Winter, "A Terracotta Griffin Head from Poggio Civitate (Murlo)," contribution to DE PUMA AND SMALL, EDS.

Index

U

V

W